# CHEETAH'S

## ULTIMATE COOKBOOK

EPIC EATS ANYONE CAN COOK

# CHEETAH'S ULTIMATE COOKBOOK

CHEETAH & GOODBOY NOAH

**Publisher** Mike Sanders
**Art & Design Director** William Thomas
**Editorial Director** Ann Barton
**Senior Editor** Molly Ahuja
**Assistant Director of Art & Design** Rebecca Batchelor
**Photographer** Stefanie Moser
**Illustrator** Debs Lim
**Developmental Editor** Melissa Haskin
**Copyeditor** Claire Safran
**Proofreader** Mira S. Park
**Recipe Tester** Alexis Winder-Daniel
**Indexer** Beverlee Day

First American Edition, 2025
Published in the United States by DK Publishing
1745 Broadway, 20th Floor, New York, NY 10019

The authorized representative in the EEA is Dorling Kindersley Verlag GmbH. Arnulfstr. 124, 80636 Munich, Germany


25 26 27 28 29 10 9 8 7 6 5 4 3 2 1
001-343731-SEP/2025



A catalog record for this book is available from the Library of Congress.
ISBN 978-0-5938-4973-6

DK books are available at special discounts when purchased in bulk for sales promotions, premiums, fund-raising, or educational use. For details, contact SpecialSales@dk.com

Printed and bound in China

**www.dk.com**

This book was made with Forest Stewardship Council™ certified paper – one small step in DK's commitment to a sustainable future.
Learn more at **www.dk.com/uk/information/sustainability**

# CONTENTS

## GOOD LUCK BEATING THIS MEAT . . . 129



## SEAFOOD 'N' STUFF . . . 153



## VEGETABLES, BUT NOT BORING . . . 177



## SWEET TREATS . . . 201

# DEAR READERS,

Indubitably, I'll admit, I'm not the best writer. Oftentimes I'll use big words I don't know to acquiesce the fact that I'm somewhat dim-witted. I tend to use commas, where they shouldn't be; and throw in semicolons because they look cool. However, when my best friend, Cheetah, asked me to write the foreword for his cookbook, I knew I had to rise to the occasion.

You see, Cheetah is always there for me whenever I call upon him. Whether I need to learn how to make a delicious lasagna, or I need his help finding buried treasure...or I fall and bump my head, which gives me amnesia so I forget how to drive and he has to teach me all over again. Cheetah has the wisdom for any occasion. *"But, how does one acquiesce such wisdom?"* is the question you're indubitably asking yourself. Well, worry not, fine reader, for the answer is simple: wisdom comes from experience. And when it comes to experience, Cheetah is never lacking. He's been all over the freakin' globe, player. I'm talking Asia, India, Vietnam...etc. You see, Cheetah's mind is a vast museum of knowledge, and it's no surprise that the most sought after exhibition in said museum... is the food one.

Indubitably, I'll admit, sometimes I feel guilty. It might be something akin to survivors' guilt. Why am I so lucky to have a best friend like Cheetah? Why am I the only one who gets to benefit firsthand from his culinary genius? Why does my life seem so awesome from the outside, but in my own mind it's a vicious hellscape like no other? Well, I believe Cheetah has found the solution, yet again, to my suffering: It is to share himself with the world. Sure Cheetah has 9 lives, but when he uses them all up, the wisdom he's acquiesced from his travels will vanish with him. So what better way to ensure his selfless legacy continues than to make this, his Ultimate Cookbook.

As I watched Cheetah type away at his typewriter with his little felt paws over the past year as he wrote this book, I would see his lifeless eyes light up as he recalled the places he's been, the people he's met, and the dishes he's perfected. It was a joy to watch my best friend relive the memories that molded him into the kitty I love so much. As I sat down and read the stories in this book and tasted the delicious food while Cheetah fervently tested each recipe, the raging storm in my mind's eye finally acquiesced into more of a light drizzle. I felt the need to thank the people, places, and cuisines that he wrote about. Because they gave everything they have to Cheetah. And trust me when I say, Cheetah gave everything he has to this book.

With love and gratitude,

**GOODBOY NOAH**

# INTRODUCTION

It was a bleak morning in autumn. I had just come out of a Zoom meeting with my soon-to-be book editor. So many publishers were on my ass to write a cookbook, throwing obscene amounts of money in my face, but I just wasn't feeling it. Was I really gonna become just another one of those highly trained chefs used as a puppet to hock regurgitated recipes to the masses? Even if I could use the money to help Noah start his frozen yogurt/sauna business, it just didn't feel like the right thing to do—yet. I needed to clear my head, so I took a stroll to the local big-box chain bookstore—a once great establishment now reserved for people who need to take a dump on their walk home from their favorite artisanal coffee shop. I admit, it had been awhile since I cracked open a cookbook myself. For one, I already know how to make just about every dish known to man. Secondly, most cookbooks are too big and heavy for my polyfill-stuffed, fabric arms. But as I perused the cookbook section, I noticed something—something highly disturbing to my feline constitution. Everything was infuriatingly regional, with titles such as "How to Make Italian Food," "How to Make Japanese Food," and "How to Make Gluten-Free, Ketogenic, Paleolithic, Vegan California Food, for Dummies." It was like being in the zoo all over again, with various culinary techniques and traditions separated much like animals in cages. The horror was too much to bear.

You see, I spent my formative years in captivity at the LA Zoo. Back then I was nothing more than an exotic attraction for drooling children and their listless parents to gawk at. But the worst part of it all—the food. The zookeepers would dole out the same food day in and day out to me and my fellow cheetahs. It was the usual slop, consisting mainly of scrap meat from the central valley slaughterhouses. Needless to say, it was some vile shit; But when that's all there is to eat, you eat it. That is until one day, after an unusually difficult time getting some gristly chuck down, I decided enough was enough. I harnessed the power of fire, and using a pit I dug with my bare paws, I smoked that chuck underground with some wild herbs I found growing in our enclosure. The scent was unbelievable, and the taste? Like nothing I'd ever experienced—somehow that tough, chewy, almost inedible piece of meat became the most delicious thing to ever grace my scratchy tongue. And as for my fellow cheetahs, they couldn't believe their stomachs. I knew right then and there, that was my true calling.

Luckily for me, a dim-witted teenager named Noah had recently won a year-long pass to the zoo in a school raffle; And man, did he put that shit to good use. That dude was at the zoo every single day, trying to reach his hands through the bars to touch the animals. I almost bit his hand off one day to teach him a lesson, but he was so naive and innocent, I figured it best if I gave him a pass. Good thing too, because that obtuse muthafucka was the key to getting out of that godforsaken hellhole.

See, when I started cooking, I would do it in the back of the enclosure so none of the zookeepers would see me. They were so preoccupied with the other animals that I managed to stay under their radar. Noah, however, stumbled upon me one day as I was glazing this veal shank with a red wine reduction, a technique I had been trying to perfect. I still don't know how he did it, but there he was, in the enclosure with me. *"So cheetahs can cook?"* he asked. *"That's pretty cool."* I jumped, shocked by the sound of a human voice so close, spilling the shank on the ground and thus ruining the dish I had been working on for the last six hours. I could go into the detailed minutiae of our conversation, but what you really need to know is that Noah, as numb-skulled as he is, has the palette of a well-seasoned chef. He told me about a place that serves a similar dish in downtown LA, a small hole-in-the-wall Italian spot he knew, and said he'd be happy to take me there. I jumped at the chance, and since he knew how to get into the enclosure without raising an alarm, I knew he could somehow break me out. We made a plan for him to come back at midnight and sneak me out of the zoo. I made sure to write down all my meat recipes to leave behind for the other cheetahs, and that night Noah and I executed my escape.

The next day he took me to the Italian spot, and it was just as good as he said it would be. From that moment on, I knew I found a best friend for life. He took me around all of his favorite spots in LA, and we tried several new ones as well. LA, being the cultural melting pot that it is, has all sorts of cuisines from all over the world, and we tried every single one we could. I was in heaven. Noah, unfortunately, has a hard time retaining most information, but I remembered every single thing we tasted and would try to recreate the recipes at our modest two-bedroom home in the valley. Those first couple of years served as a culinary boot camp in some ways; But eventually, I felt like I soaked up as much knowledge as I could. I was like a butterfly that outgrew the confines of its cocoon. It was time I broke out of Southern California and spread my wings. I was determined to taste what the world had to offer.

I bid farewell to Noah, and after I finally got him to stop crying, I was on my way. My first stop—Mexico City. I tasted the plethora of flavors the Yucateco, Oaxaceño and Poblano cuisines have to offer. I took what I learned there and kept my travels going, hopping from country to country, continent to continent. You name it, I went there; Southern France, Tuscany, Greece, Turkey, Morocco, China, Japan, India, Colombia—the list goes on and on, and with every stop along the way, my understanding of flavors and the people behind them grew. I was gone for 2 years, and as much as I loved traveling and seeing the world, I was itching to get back to my best friend.

As soon as I got home, I began cooking up a storm. I showed Noah everything I learned abroad, recounting tales of exotic cuisines and women. Around that time, Noah just so happened to be throwing in the towel on his R&B music career. I confessed to him that I felt guilty. I thought that maybe if I was around, I could have helped him out, especially given my previous musical experience at the zoo with my rap group Beast Reality (shout out to Dr. Shellz and Killah C). Little did I know, Noah had something else up his sleeve. One day over breakfast, Noah exclaimed, *"Cheetah! I have a new idea to combine both of our greatest skills and solidify our bond of friendship for eternity!"*

*"Damn, bro, what is it?"*, I asked. His reply: *"We're gonna make an omelette...to music."* And the rest is history. Since January 2022, Noah and I have been offering up my cooking techniques to the masses, and it has been one of the most rewarding adventures of my life.

I returned home from the bookstore that bleak autumn day, still at a loss for what to do. I saw that Noah had brought in the mail, and as I flipped through my stack, one envelope in particular called out to me. It had scratches all over it and nearly illegible handwriting on the front. I opened it up to find a photo and a letter. The photo was of my old pride of cheetahs at the LA Zoo enclosure, having what looked like the most fun barbeque any non-human has ever had. I read the letter. It was a sweet, heartfelt thank you for leaving behind my recipes, allowing my old family to build off of what I'd started. Those simple recipes, the origin to what became my true calling, was adding real value to their lives.

That's when it hit me. I simply *had* to write this book. If my recipes could make a difference to them, imagine what they could do for the rest of the world. Suddenly, not making this book for the people sounded like a mortal sin. But what to share? Where to start? Do I write a collection of recipes from my time in SoCal? Or Italy? Maybe Central America? Asia perhaps? Nah, man. Fuck all that. I wanted this book to be real—a reflection of my entire journey up until now. I looked back and realized I could never write a boring ass, regional collection of recipes, because I just don't think of food that way. That's not how I discovered my love of cooking. That's not my story. My story is one of adversity, adventure, dedication, love, triumph and most importantly, friendship. And honestly, my story isn't even my own. To me, it's also the stories of everyone I've ever met, because without them, I simply wouldn't be anything close to the Cheetah I am today. So I hopped on another zoom with those muthafuckas at DK, and I agreed to make this book—a culinary memoir of sorts, sharing with you my travels and the dishes I encountered and perfected along the way. So, without further adieu, It is my honor to humbly set these recipes free. I hope they enhance your life and kitchen as they did mine.

# THE PANTRY OF YOUR DREAMS

**Look, we all have our kitchen ride-or-dies—the ingredients we know will always deliver. Since I'm handing over a bunch of my recipes, it only feels right to share my personal pantry MVPs. These are the staples that keep my kitchen (and my stomach) happy.**

## CANNED GOODS & SHELF-STABLE LIQUIDS

- **San Marzano Canned Tomatoes:** A canned tomato is not *just* a canned tomato. San Marzanos are the Beyoncé of the tomato world—next-level. Look for Cento, Bianco di Napoli, or Mutti for tomato sauce supremacy.
- **Canned Coconut Milk:** This creamy, dreamy milk is essential for curries, soups, or turning your coffee into a tropical vacation. I keep a few cans on paw at all times.
- **Dark Soy Sauce:** Think of dark soy sauce as the brooding, mysterious sibling of light soy. It's rich, deep, and makes everything taste like it came from a restaurant. Don't sleep on light soy sauce—it's a kitchen staple, too—but when you want that next-level flavor bomb, dark soy is the move.
- **Fish Sauce:** Just a few drops, and BAM! You're in umami town. Use sparingly, though—a little can go a long way.
- **Hot Sauce:** Pick your poison—Sriracha, Cholula, or something with a label that screams "Beware". They're all welcome in my pantry.
- **Canned Beans:** Black, kidney, or cannellini—great for lazy days when you need protein fast.

## GRAINS, LEGUMES & STARCHES

- **Rice:** Jasmine, basmati, or short-grain—there's a rice for every occasion.
- **Quinoa:** For when you want to feel healthy and trendy at the same time.
- **Grits:** Comfort food at its finest. If you've never had cheesy grits, we can't be friends.
- **Rolled Oats:** Breakfast, cookies, or a crunchy crumble topping—oats are the Swiss Army knife of grains.
- **Dried Garbanzo Beans (Chickpeas):** Want to impress people with the silkiest hummus of their lives? Start with dried chickpeas. Canned works in a pinch, but dried is the real MVP.
- **Tubers:** Potatoes, sweet potatoes, and yams: the versatile, carb-loaded heroes of your pantry. Keep them cool and dark, and they'll stick around longer than your last houseplant.

## BAKING & COOKING ESSENTIALS

- **Flour:** All-purpose for everything, bread flour for when you're making bread. Pro tip: Good flour = better food.
- **Yeast:** Got a pizza night or bread-making dream? Yeast is your new bestie.

- **Baking Powder:** The unsung hero of fluffy pancakes, towering cakes, and biscuits that make you feel like you're living your best Southern grandma life. Just make sure it's fresh—expired baking powder is basically kitchen dust.
- **Panko Bread Crumbs:** The crunchy upgrade your fried foods didn't know they needed.
- **Butter:** Grass-fed butter is the flavor-packed fatty friend every dish deserves. Try Kerrygold or Le Beurre Bordier, and never look back.
- **Extra-Virgin Olive Oil:** EVOO is the crown jewel of drizzles. It'll make your salads sing and your garnishes glow.
- **High-Temperature Oil:** Avocado oil if you're feeling bougie; canola or peanut oil otherwise.
- **Honey:** Real, single-source honey only. Anything else is a crime against bees.
- **Maple Syrup:** If it's not from Canada or Vermont, we don't want it.
- **Sugar:** Brown and granulated—sweeten your marinades, your cookies, and your life.

## SPICES, HERBS & FLAVOR BOOSTERS

- **Dried Spices:** Stock up on the basics (rosemary, thyme, oregano) and spice it up with smoked paprika, cayenne, turmeric, cinnamon, and bay leaves.
- **Dried Chilis:** Toast these bad boys to unlock a whole new world of smoky heat.
- **Salts:** Cooking salt, brining salt, and fancy finishing salt (Maldon, I see you). Yes, you want all three.
- **Pepper:** Black is the everyday MVP; white is for when you're feeling like a French chef.
- **Tahini:** Nutty, creamy, and perfect for hummus or a killer salad dressing.

## VINEGARS & ACIDS

- **Vinegars:** Regular balsamic, aged balsamic, white balsamic, rice, apple cider, and sherry—because sometimes your dish just needs a little tang.
- **Citrus:** Lemons and oranges brighten dishes, look cute on the counter, and make you feel like a regular Martha Stewart.

## CHEESES

- **Parmigiano Reggiano:** The OG cheese royalty. It's pricey, but it's worth it.

## STOCKS & BROTHS

- **Stocks:** Keep vegetable or chicken stock on hand to save your sauces and soups. Bouillon cubes or paste are great if you're short on space.

## NUTS & SEEDS

- **Nuts & Seeds:** Almonds, walnuts, sesame seeds, and sunflower seeds. Toast them for extra flavor and watch your salads and sauces level up.

## PASTA

- **Pasta:** Bucatini for creamy sauces, pappardelle for pesto, and linguine or spaghetti for bolognese. Barilla is solid, but artisan pastas are a flex worth trying.

## MIREPOIX (VEGETABLES)

- **Carrots, Onions & Celery:** The holy trinity of cooking. If you don't have these in your kitchen, are you even trying?

# BREAKFAST BANGERS

# NUTTY-ASS HOMEMADE GRANOLA

Serves 12 • Prep Time: 10 minutes • Cook Time: 30 minute • Total Time: 40 minutes

My Nutty-Ass Homemade Granola—a breakfast so outrageously good, it should probably come with a warning label. This granola is so addictive, you'll find yourself face-deep in the jar, spoon in hand, hoping no one's watching as you devour it like a ravenous raccoon. Whether you're trying to impress your significant other, or just need a crunchy fix that doesn't judge you for your life choices, this granola has got you covered. So pour yourself a bowl, add some milk, and embrace a breakfast that's as unapologetically bold as you are. Just try not to eat the whole batch in one sitting like Noah's no-self-control-having ass.

## INGREDIENTS

3 cups rolled (old-fashioned) oats
1 cup raw cashews, chopped
1 cup raw hazelnuts, chopped
½ cup raw pumpkin seeds
1 cup unsweetened coconut flakes
⅓ cup honey or maple syrup
¼ cup coconut oil
1 teaspoon vanilla extract
½ teaspoon ground cinnamon
¼ teaspoon salt
1 cup dried fruit of choice, such as raisins, cranberries, or chopped apricots (optional)

## METHOD

1. Preheat your oven to 325°F (160°C). Line a large baking sheet with parchment paper or a silicone baking mat.
2. In a big ass mixing bowl, combine the rolled oats, cashews, hazelnuts, pumpkin seeds, and coconut flakes. Stir to combine.
3. In a small saucepan over low heat, combine the honey or maple syrup, coconut oil, vanilla extract, cinnamon, and salt. Cook, stirring frequently, until the mixture is well combined and the coconut oil is fully melted.
4. Pour the wet ingredients into the bowl with the dry ingredients. Use a spatula or wooden spoon to mix everything together until the oats and nuts are evenly coated.
5. Spread the oat mixture in an even layer on the prepared baking sheet. Bake for 25 to 30 minutes, stirring halfway through, until the granola is golden brown and crispy.
6. If using dried fruit, remove the baking sheet from the oven and sprinkle the dried fruit over the hot granola. Gently stir to combine.
7. Allow the granola to cool completely on the baking sheet. It will continue to crisp up as it cools.
8. Once cooled, transfer the granola to an airtight container or glass jar for storage. It will keep for up to 2 weeks at room temperature. Serve with yogurt or milk and fresh berries.

## CHEETAH'S SECRET

MAKE EASY PARFAIT CUPS! USING 8-OUNCE CUPS OR JARS, FILL THE BOTTOM WITH 2 TABLESPOONS OF YOUR FAVORITE FRUIT JAM, THEN SPOON IN 4 TO 5 OUNCES OF YOGURT AND STORE IN THE FRIDGE FOR UP TO 4 DAYS. TOP WITH THE HOMEMADE GRANOLA WHEN YOU'RE READY TO SERVE.

# EASY-ASS OVERNIGHT OATS

Serves 2 • Prep Time: 5 minutes • Cook Time: None • Total Time: 5 minutes (plus 8 hours for soaking)

**If breakfast is the most important meal of the day, why not start it with something that's as effortless as hitting the snooze button? Enter: Easy-ass Overnight Oats. This recipe is so simple, it practically makes itself while you're dreaming about winning the lottery (or just getting five more minutes of sleep). Perfect for busy mornings where you need a grab-and-go breakfast. These oats are a lifesaver, giving you a nutritious start without the morning chaos. Plus, they're endlessly customizable so you can keep breakfast interesting without needing a bougie-ass culinary degree. Just mix, refrigerate, and wake up to breakfast bliss. It's like magic, but with oats.**

## INGREDIENTS

½ cup rolled (old-fashioned) oats

½ cup Greek yogurt (any brand or fat percentage)

½ cup whole milk, almond milk, or soy milk

1 tablespoon honey (or your favorite sweetener like agave nectar or maple syrup)

¼ cup fresh blueberries (or frozen, thawed)

Optional toppings: blueberries, sliced almonds, honey

### SPECIAL EQUIPMENT

2× 16-ounce Mason jars with lids

## METHOD

1. In each jar, combine half of the rolled oats, Greek yogurt, milk, and honey. Stir until well combined. The honey should be evenly distributed.
2. Use a spoon to gently stir in the blueberries (see Note).
3. Screw on the lids and refrigerate overnight or for at least 6 to 8 hours. This allows the oats to soak up the liquid and soften while the flavors meld together.
4. Give the oats a good stir. If the mixture seems too thick, you can add a splash of milk.
5. Serve with extra blueberries, sliced almonds, or a drizzle of honey, if desired.
6. Grab a spoon and enjoy!

***Note:** If you're using frozen blueberries, drain any excess liquid before adding to the oats.*

## CHEETAH'S SECRET VARIATIONS

### MANGO-COCONUT OVERNIGHT OATS

Follow the same instructions as the original recipe but swap the blueberries with ¼ cup diced mango and use coconut milk instead of regular milk. Top with shredded coconut and sliced almonds!

### CHOCOLATE-BANANA OVERNIGHT OATS

For a decadent breakfast treat follow the original recipe but add 1 tablespoon of cocoa powder and 1 mashed banana to the oat mixture. Serve topped with sliced bananas and chocolate chips!

### RASPBERRY-ALMOND OVERNIGHT OATS

Follow the original recipe but replace the blueberries with ¼ cup of fresh raspberries and add 2 tablespoons of sliced almonds to the oat mixture. Serve topped with extra raspberries and a drizzle of almond butter.

# LITTLE-ASS MUFFIN TIN EGG BITES

Serves 6 • Prep Time: 7 minutes • Cook Time: 20 minutes • Total Time: 27 minutes

Say good morning to some Little-Ass Muffin Tin Egg Bites, the tiny breakfast heroes you never knew you needed. These mini marvels pack a punch of flavor in a bite-sized package, proving once and for all that good things do come in small packages. Perfect for meal prepping, these egg bites are like your morning's personal cheerleaders, ready to fuel your day with protein and deliciousness. Customize them with your favorite veggies, cheese, and meats—or keep them simple, because let's face it, they're dope on their own. Pop them in the oven, let them puff up tall, and enjoy a breakfast that's as convenient as it is adorable. Perfect for on-the-go mornings or anytime you need a little extra somethin' yummy, healthy, and packed with protein.

## INGREDIENTS

- 6 large eggs
- ¼ cup milk such as whole milk, almond milk, or soy milk
- Salt and pepper, to taste
- ⅓ cup crumbled feta cheese
- ¼ cup pitted Kalamata olives, chopped
- 4 slices cooked bacon, chopped
- ½ cup fresh asparagus, ends trimmed and chopped into small pieces
- Cooking spray or melted butter, for greasing

### SPECIAL EQUIPMENT

12-cup muffin pan

## METHOD

1. Preheat the oven to 350°F (175°C).
2. Grease a 12-cup muffin pan with cooking spray or melted butter.
3. In a large bowl, whisk together the eggs and milk until well combined. Season with salt and pepper to taste.
4. Divide the feta cheese, Kalamata olives, bacon, and asparagus evenly among the muffin cups.
5. Fill each cup about two-thirds of the way full with the egg mixture.
6. Bake for 18 to 20 minutes, or until the eggs are set and lightly golden on top.
7. Allow the egg bites to cool in the pan for a few minutes. Use a knife or spatula to loosen the edges and remove them from the cups. Serve warm. (See Cheetah's Secret)

## CHEETAH'S SECRET

IF YOU ARE MEAL PREPPING, ALLOW THE BITES TO COOL TO ROOM TEMPERATURE, THEN STORE IN AN AIRTIGHT CONTAINER IN THE REFRIGERATOR FOR UP TO 4 DAYS. TO REHEAT, POP THESE BAD BOYS IN THE MICROWAVE ON HIGH FOR 30 SECONDS OR THROW THEM IN AN AIR FRYER SET TO 375°F (190°C) FOR 2–3 MINUTES.

YOU CAN SUBSTITUTE DIFFERENT TYPES OF CHEESE, SUCH AS GOAT CHEESE OR CHEDDAR, AND ADD ADDITIONAL VEGETABLES OR HERBS FOR EVEN MORE FLAVOR.

# "CHALLA BACK" FRENCH-ASS TOAST

Serves **2 to 3** • Prep Time: **6 minutes** • Cook Time: **18 minutes** • Total Time: **24 minutes**

**This delightful twist on a classic uses that rich, eggy challah bread we all know and love and turns your morning meal into a culinary mitzvah. Crispy on the outside, fluffy on the inside, and so delicious it might just make you break into a hora right at the breakfast table. Mazel tov, Muthafucka. This French toast is your ticket to breakfast nirvana.**

## INGREDIENTS

4 large eggs

1 cup whole milk

¼ cup heavy cream

2 tablespoons granulated sugar

1 teaspoon vanilla extract

½ teaspoon ground cinnamon

Pinch of salt

1 loaf of challah bread, sliced into thick slices (about 1-inch (2½ cm) thick)

Butter or neutral oil, for cooking

### FOR SERVING

Maple syrup

Powdered sugar

Fresh berries

## METHOD

1. Preheat a griddle or large skillet over medium heat. Meanwhile, in a large shallow bowl or pie plate, whisk together the eggs, milk, heavy cream, sugar, vanilla extract, cinnamon, and salt until well combined.
2. Working in batches of 2 to 3 slices, dip each slice of challah into the egg mixture, ensuring that both sides are coated evenly. Let the bread soak for 1 to 2 minutes per side, allowing it to absorb the liquid without becoming too soggy.
3. Add a small amount of butter or oil to coat the preheated griddle or skillet. Place the soaked challah slices onto the hot surface and cook until golden brown and crisp on both sides, 3 to 4 minutes per side.
4. As you cook the French toast, you can keep the cooked slices warm in a low-temp oven (200°F [95°C]) on a baking sheet lined with parchment paper while you finish cooking the remaining slices.
5. Once all the French toast slices are cooked, transfer them to serving plates. Serve with maple syrup, a dusting of powdered sugar, and fresh berries on top for an extra touch of decadence.
6. Dive into this indulgent breakfast delight and savor every delicious bite!

## CHEETAH'S SECRET

FEEL FREE TO CUSTOMIZE THIS RECIPE TO YOUR LIKING BY ADDING A SPRINKLE OF NUTMEG AND ORANGE ZEST TO THE EGG MIXTURE, OR BY TOPPING THE FRENCH TOAST WITH WHIPPED CREAM OR A DOLLOP OF GREEK YOGURT MIXED WITH A TOUCH OF HONEY.

# LEMONY-ASS RICOTTA PANCAKES

## with Blueberry Cardamom Sauce

Serves 4 • Prep Time: 5 minutes • Cook Time: 10 minutes • Total Time: 15 minutes

**Get ready to up your breakfast game with these Lemon-Ricotta Pancakes. These fluffy-ass flapjacks are the brunch equivalent of sunshine on a plate, brightened with a zesty lemon kick that'll wake up your taste buds faster than a double shot of espresso. The secret weapon? Ricotta cheese—it makes these pancakes light, creamy, and perfectly textured. Serve them with my special Blueberry Cardamom sauce for a breakfast guaranteed to stunt on any guest.**

### INGREDIENTS

1 cup all-purpose flour
1 tablespoon granulated sugar
1 teaspoon baking powder
½ teaspoon baking soda
¼ teaspoon salt
½ cup ricotta cheese
⅔ cup milk
1 large egg
Zest of 1 lemon
2 tablespoons fresh lemon juice
Butter or oil, for cooking
Maple syrup and fresh berries, for serving (optional)

#### BLUEBERRY CARDAMOM SAUCE

2 cups fresh or frozen blueberries
⅓ cup granulated sugar (plus more, to taste)
½ teaspoon ground cardamom
1 teaspoon lemon juice
1 teaspoon cornstarch mixed with 2 teaspoons water (to make a slurry)

### METHOD

1. Preheat the oven to 200°F (90°C).
2. In a large ass bowl, whisk together the flour, sugar, baking powder, baking soda, and salt until well combined.
3. In another large bowl, whisk together the ricotta cheese, milk, egg, lemon zest, and lemon juice until smooth.
4. Pour the wet ingredients into the dry ingredients and gently stir until just combined. Be careful not to overmix. A few lumps in the batter are okay.
5. Heat a nonstick griddle or large skillet over medium heat. Add a small amount of butter or oil to grease the surface.
6. Pour ¼ cup of batter onto the hot griddle for each pancake. Leave enough room for the batter to spread. You may need to work in batches. Cook until bubbles form and the edges look set, about 2 to 3 minutes. Flip and cook for an additional 1 to 2 minutes, or until golden brown and cooked through.
7. Keep warm in the oven on a baking tray or ovenproof plate.
8. To make the sauce: In a medium saucepan, combine the blueberries, sugar, ¼ cup water, and cardamom. Bring it to a simmer over medium heat, stirring occasionally, until the blueberries start to release their sweet, sweet juices (about 5 minutes).
9. Stir in the lemon juice.
10. Slowly pour in the cornstarch slurry, stirring constantly to avoid lumps.
11. Continue to simmer for 2 to 3 minutes or until the sauce thickens enough to coat the back of a spoon.
12. Remove the sauce from the heat and let it cool slightly before serving over your lemon ricotta pancakes.

# AMERICAN-ASS BREAKFAST PLATTER

Serves 4 • Prep Time: 5 minutes • Cook Time: 25 minutes • Total Time: 30 minutes

Get ready to tackle the morning like a true patriot with this American-Ass Breakfast Platter. But don't get it twisted—this isn't just your average greasy spoon diner spread. This is a love letter to everything we adore about breakfast, dialed up to eleven. With my peppery maple bacon and my perfect, pillowy eggs, your palate will be pledging allegiance to this dish. Whether you're a cowboy fueling up for a day on the ranch or just someone who appreciates some good ol' American indulgence, this platter's your ticket to a star-spangled morning. God bless America and God bless this breakfast.

## INGREDIENTS

### CHEETAH'S MAGIC MAPLE PEPPER BACON

- 16 slices thick-cut bacon
- 2 tablespoons maple syrup
- Freshly ground black pepper, to taste

### PERFECTLY CRISPY HASH BROWNS

- 2 large Russet Burbank potatoes
- 2 tablespoons ghee
- Salt and pepper, to taste

### PILLOWY SCRAMBLED EGGS

- 2 tablespoons salted butter, divided
- 8 large eggs
- 3 tablespoons heavy cream
- 1 tablespoon chopped chives, plus extra for garnish
- Salt and freshly ground black pepper, to taste

### FOR ASSEMBLY

- 8 slices of bread, such as sourdough or whole wheat
- Sliced avocado, halved cherry tomatoes, sautéed spinach, ketchup, or hot sauce, for serving (optional)

## CHEETAH'S MAGIC MAPLE PEPPER BACON

TRY THIS!

1. Preheat the oven to 400°F (200°C) and line a baking sheet with parchment paper.
2. Place the bacon slices in a single layer on the prepared baking sheet. Bake that shit for 12 to 15 minutes, or until the bacon is just beginning to crisp. Remove the tray from the oven.
3. Flip each piece of bacon, brush with that sweet maple syrup, and sprinkle with freshly ground black pepper. Put it back in the oven and cook for 5 more minutes or until crispy and deep brown in color. Then set it aside.

## PERFECTLY CRISPY HASH BROWNS

1. Grate the potatoes on the large side of a box grater, then transfer the grated potato to a clean tea towel or cheesecloth and squeeze out as much moisture as possible.
2. Transfer the grated potato to a mixing bowl and season with salt and pepper.
3. Melt the ghee in a large cast-iron skillet over medium-low heat. Add the potatoes to the skillet, spreading them out into an even layer. Use a spatula to press down on the potatoes until flattened.
4. Cook, undisturbed, for 5 to 7 minutes, or until golden brown and crispy on one side. Working in sections, use a spatula to flip the hash browns over. Cook for 5 to 7 additional minutes, or until both sides are golden brown and crispy.

## PILLOWY SCRAMBLED EGGS

1 Place a big ass skillet over medium heat and add the butter.

2 Crack the eggs into a large mixing bowl and add the cream and chives. Whisk that shit until it's fully combined and frothy.

3 Pour the eggs into the skillet and stir every few seconds so that the egg doesn't brown. Cook for 3 to 5 minutes or until the eggs are done to your liking.

4 Sprinkle with salt and pepper to taste and stir one more time so it's evenly seasoned.

5 Garnish with extra chopped chives.

## ASSEMBLY

1 While the eggs are cooking, toast the bread until golden brown. Spread the remaining tablespoon of butter on the toasted bread, if desired.

2 Place 2 slices of bacon, a quarter of the eggs, hashbrowns, and toast on each dish and serve. If desired, add optional toppings such as sliced avocado, halved cherry tomatoes, or sautéed spinach to the platter for extra flavor and nutrition and serve with your favorite condiments such as ketchup or hot sauce.

# FULL-ASS ENGLISH BREAKFAST

Serves **2** • Prep Time: **5 minutes** • Cook Time: **30 minutes** • Total Time: **35 minutes**

**Rise and shine, mate! Put on the kettle and get ready because this English Breakfast is here to give your morning a proper British kick in the trousers. This epic morning feast would make even the queen proud, God rest her soul. We're talking rashers of English bacon, sizzling sausages, perfectly fried eggs, baked beans, grilled tomatoes, and mushrooms, all cozying up on your plate to warm you up like a fireplace on a rainy London day. And don't forget the toast and black pudding—it's a full English, after all, you bloody wankers! This hearty spread is perfect for those mornings when you need more than just a cuppa tea to get you going. Cheerio!**

## INGREDIENTS

Butter, for frying

4 breakfast pork sausage links

4 slices English bacon (see Cheetah's Secrets)

2 slices black pudding (optional, see Notes)

1 slice black pudding (optional, see Notes)

1 cup baby bella mushrooms, sliced

5 to 7 on-the-vine cherry tomatoes

1× 13.7 ounce (390g) can Heinz Baked Beans

1 potato, peeled and grated

Salt and pepper, to taste

4 large eggs

2 slices white bread, for toasting

## METHOD

1. Heat a big ass frying pan over medium heat. Add a little bit of butter and the sausages and cook, turning frequently, until browned and cooked through, 10 to 15 minutes. Remove and keep warm on a plate covered in foil.
2. In the same pan you used for the sausages, add the bacon. Cook until almost crispy, 2 to 3 minutes per side, then transfer to the same plate with the sausages to keep warm. English bacon is NOT supposed to be crispy. That's just how it is.
3. Cook slices of black pudding in the same skillet as the bacon for 3 to 4 minutes on each side until browned. Remove and keep warm with the sausages and bacon.
4. Add a bit more butter to the pan, if needed. Add the sliced mushrooms and cook, stirring often, until browned and soft, about 8 minutes. Push the mushrooms to one side and add the tomatoes. Cook, stirring occasionally, until the skins begin to brown and the fruit softens, but not so much that they burst open. Remove and keep warm with the sausages, bacon, and black pudding.
5. Heat the baked beans in a small saucepan over low heat, stirring occasionally.
6. In a separate large frying pan, heat a small amount of butter or oil over medium heat. Add the grated potato, and press it down with a spatula to flatten that shit. Cook for 5 to 8 minutes per side, until golden and crispy. Season with salt and pepper. Transfer the hash browns to a plate and a cover with foil to keep warm.
7. In the same pan as the hash browns, add a bit of butter and fry the eggs to your liking. Season with salt and pepper.

8 Toast the slices of bread and butter them generously.

9 Arrange the sausages, bacon, mushrooms, tomatoes, baked beans, hash browns, eggs, and toast among two large plates.

10 Serve with a cup of strong tea, because what's a full English breakfast without it?

## CHEETAH'S SECRETS

ENGLISH BACON TAKES A DIFFERENT APPROACH THAN THE STREAKY, CRISPY AMERICAN KIND. CUT FROM THE PIG'S LOIN, IT'S LEANER, MEATIER, AND HAS A MORE ROBUST TEXTURE, THOUGH IT DOESN'T CRISP UP QUITE THE SAME. YOU CAN USUALLY AND IT IN HIGH-END GROCERY STORES OR SPECIALTY BUTCHER SHOPS. IF IT'S NOT AVAILABLE, CANADIAN BACON MAKES A SOLID SUBSTITUTE, OFFERING THE SAME LEAN, LOIN-CUT QUALITY.

DON'T LET THE NAME FOOL YOU—BLACK PUDDING ISN'T PUDDING AT ALL. LIKE MANY ODDLY NAMED BRITISH FOODS, IT'S A LITTLE MISLEADING. IT'S ACTUALLY A TYPE OF BLOOD SAUSAGE WITH DEEP ROOTS IN ENGLISH AND IRISH CULINARY TRADITIONS, AND IT'S FREAKIN' DELICIOUS WHEN YOU FRY IT UP.

# DECADENT-ASS PROSCIUTTO EGGS BENEDICT

Serves 2 • Prep Time: 10 minutes • Cook Time: 10 minutes • Total Time: 20 minutes

**Prepare to indulge in breakfast luxury with this Decadent-Ass Prosciutto Eggs Benedict. This isn't just any eggs benedict—this one took a vacation to Italy and came back with a taste for the finer things in life. Imagine velvety poached eggs nestled on delicate slices of prosciutto, sitting on buttery, pillowy brioche, all draped in rich, silky hollandaise sauce. I mean, shit, if this dish isn't the epitome of daytime decadence, I don't know what it is. Perfect for impressing guests at brunch or treating yourself to a lavish start to the day, you can't go wrong with this eggs benny.**

## INGREDIENTS

### HOLLANDAISE SAUCE

½ cup butter
4 large egg yolks
1 tablespoon lemon juice
½ teaspoon Dijon mustard

### BENEDICT

2 tablespoons white vinegar
3 large egg yolks
4 slices of brioche bread, toasted
8 slices of prosciutto
Salt and pepper, to taste
Pinch of cayenne pepper or paprika (optional)
Chopped fresh chives or chopped curly-leaf parsley, for garnish (optional)
Salt and pepper, to taste

### SPECIAL EQUIPMENT

Blender

## METHOD

### FOR THE HOLLANDAISE SAUCE

1 Melt the butter in a small saucepan over low heat. Set aside to cool slightly.

2 Add the egg yolks, lemon juice, and Dijon mustard to the base of a blender. Blend it up on low until well combined, 45 seconds or so.

3 With the blender running on low speed, slowly pour that melted butter into the egg yolk mixture in a steady stream. Continue blending until the mixture thickens to a nice and creamy consistency. At this point, the sauce should be smooth and glossy as hell.

4 Season with salt and pepper. If you so desire, add a pinch of cayenne pepper or paprika for a subtle kick of flavor.

5 If the hollandaise sauce is too thick, you can thin it out by adding a teaspoon of warm water and blending. Repeat, if necessary, until you reach your desired consistency.

### FOR THE BENEDICT

TRY THIS!

6 Fill a large, deep skillet or saucepan with enough water to cover the eggs by 2 inches (5 cm) and bring it to a gentle simmer over medium heat. Add the vinegar to the water (this helps the eggs hold their shape).

7 Crack each egg into a small bowl or ramekin. Stir the water in one direction using a wooden spoon. A gentle whirlpool should form. Carefully slide 1 egg into the center of the whirlpool. Repeat with the remaining eggs. Cook the eggs for about 3 to 4 minutes, or until the whites are set but the yolks are still runny.

8 Using a slotted spoon, carefully remove the poached eggs from the water and transfer them to a paper towel-lined plate. Season with salt and pepper.

9 Divide the brioche between 4 plates, placing 1 slice on each plate. Add 2 slices of prosciutto to each piece of toast, then one egg. Spoon hollandaise sauce generously over each poached egg.

10 Sprinkle chopped fresh chives or parsley over the eggs benedict for a pop of color and extra flavor.

11 Serve the Decadent-ass Prosciutto Eggs Benedict immediately and enjoy!

## CHEETAH'S SECRET

**PUT YOUR OWN SPIN ON THIS RECIPE BY ADDING SLICED AVOCADO, ROASTED TOMATOES, OR SAUTÉED SPINACH. OR CHANGE UP THE MEAT BY USING BACON, SMOKED SALMON, OR SAUTÉED MUSHROOMS INSTEAD OF THE PROSCIUTTO.**

# TURKISH-ASS EGGS

Serves 2 • Prep Time: 7 minutes • Cook Time: 10 minutes • Total Time: 17 minutes

**Spice up your morning with some Turkish eggs, a breakfast that's got more flair than a belly dancer at the bazaar. This dish is a blend of poached eggs floating on a bed of garlicky yogurt, all drizzled with sizzling hot chili butter. It'll be like your taste buds took a trip to Istanbul and came back with a suitcase full of flavor. So break out the spices, grab some crusty bread for dipping, and get ready for a breakfast that's as bold and beautiful as Fatma, the fine-ass Turkish woman who taught me this recipe (along with some other things I can't mention at this time). Afiyet olsun!**

## INGREDIENTS

1 cup plain Greek yogurt
2 garlic cloves, minced
Salt, to taste
4 large eggs
2 tablespoons unsalted butter
1 teaspoon Aleppo pepper flakes (or to taste)
Fresh flat-leaf parsley, chopped
Sourdough bread or crusty bread, for serving (optional)

## METHOD

1. In a small bowl, whisk together the Greek yogurt and minced garlic until silky smooth. Season with salt to taste. Divide the yogurt mixture between two serving plates, spreading it out into a thin layer.
2. Bring a large pot of water to a gentle simmer over medium heat. Crack each egg into a small bowl or ramekin. Stir the water in one direction using a wooden spoon. A gentle whirlpool should form. Carefully slide 1 egg into the center of the whirlpool. Repeat with the remaining eggs. Cook the eggs for about 3 to 4 minutes, or until the whites are set but the yolks are still runny. Use a slotted spoon to remove the poached eggs from the water and to drain any excess water.
3. Carefully place 2 poached eggs on top of each portion of yogurt.
4. In a small saucepan, melt the butter over low heat. Once melted, add the Aleppo pepper flakes and stir to combine. Cook for about 1 minute, stirring constantly, until the butter is fragrant and the pepper flakes are evenly distributed.
5. Drizzle the Aleppo pepper–infused butter over the poached eggs and yogurt.
6. Sprinkle with freshly chopped parsley and serve immediately, accompanied by slices of sourdough bread for dipping.
7. Enjoy!

# BREAKFAST-ASS BURRITO

Serves 4 • Prep Time: 5 minutes • Cook Time: 20 minute • Total Time: 25 minutes

**Start your day off right with the perfect Breakfast-Ass Burrito, featuring a homemade pico de gallo that's so fresh and flavorful, it might just be the secret to world peace. This zesty salsa is loaded with ripe, juicy tomatoes, and a kick of lime that'll wake you right up. Paired with a hearty, breakfast-packed burrito filled with scrambled eggs, crispy bacon, and gooey cheese, this dish is heaven in a tortilla.**

## INGREDIENTS

### BURRITO

4 burrito-sized (10-inch [25 cm]) flour tortillas

8 slices bacon

6 large eggs, beaten

1 cup shredded cheddar or Monterey Jack cheese

Salt and pepper, to taste

1 ripe avocado, peeled, pitted, and sliced

Homemade Pico de Gallo (recipe below)

Sour cream, hot sauce, and chopped cilantro, for serving (optional)

### PICO DE GALLO

2 medium tomatoes, diced

½ small red onion, finely chopped

1 jalapeño, seeded and finely chopped

¼ cup chopped fresh cilantro

Juice of 1 lime

Salt and pepper, to taste

## METHOD

1. Make the Pico de Gallo: In a bigass bowl, combine the tomatoes, onion, jalapeño, and cilantro. Add the lime juice and season with salt and pepper to taste. Stir that shit until combined.
2. Make the burrito: In a large skillet over medium heat, cook the bacon until crispy. Transfer to a paper towel–lined plate. Allow to cool for 5 to 10 minutes, then chop it up.
3. In the same skillet over medium heat, add the eggs to that glorious bacon grease, and cook to your desired doneness. Season with salt and pepper to taste.
4. Warm up the flour tortillas in a dry skillet or microwave until warm but still pliable.
5. Divide the scrambled eggs evenly among the warmed tortillas. Top with shredded cheese, bacon, sliced avocado, and a spoonful of your delicious Pico de Gallo.
6. Fold the sides of each tortilla over the filling, then tightly roll from the bottom, tucking the sides in as you go. Place face down (seam-side down, not your face) in the hot skillet and cook for 1 to 2 minutes on each side or until golden brown.
7. Serve with your favorite toppings such as sour cream, your favorite hot sauce, or fresh cilantro.

## CHEETAH'S SECRET

YOU CAN ADD ANYTHING YOUR HEART DESIRES TO THIS BURRITO TO SHAKE UP THE FLAVOR. I LIKE TO SUBSTITUTE THE BACON WITH CHORIZO OR CHICKEN SAUSAGE, OR SOMETIMES I MAKE A VEGETARIAN VERSION WITH PORTOBELLO MUSHROOMS.

CHEETA
SALSA

## CHEETAH'S SECRET

I LIKE TO TOP MY BAGEL WITH FLAVORED CREAM CHEESE. MY FAVORITE ADD-INS ARE SCALLIONS AND GARLIC, BUT ALL SORTS OF COMBINATIONS WORK. FOR INSTANCE, NOAH LOVES HONEY-CARDAMOM CREAM CHEESE (ADD 1 TABLESPOON HONEY AND 1 TEASPOON GROUND CARDAMOM TO 8 OUNCES (227G) OF SOFTENED CREAM CHEESE. FOLLOW YOUR HEART AND YOU'LL DO NO WRONG!

### EASY SCALLION CREAM CHEESE

Mix 8 ounces (227g) of softened cream cheese with finely chopped scallions and a squeeze of lemon juice for a perfect scallion cream cheese! Add one clove of freshly crushed garlic if you want even more deliciousness.

# CANADIAN-ASS MONTREAL BAGEL

Serves 10 • Prep Time: 30 minutes • Cook Time: 25 minutes •
Total Time: 55 minutes (plus 45 minutes for rising and 10 minutes for resting)

**Oh, Canada! Get ready to experience bagel heaven with these Montreal-style bagels. These aren't just any bagels, they're the crispy, sweet, holier version of the bagel you know from the grocery store. While other bagels might take a dip in boring old water, these bagels are boiled in honey-sweetened H2O, which gives them a subtly sweet taste – kinda like Sophie, the beautiful Montreal-based-bagel-baker who showed me her secret recipe along with some other secrets a gentle-cheetah should never tell. There's nothing like the taste of these bagels to bring me right back to those simpler times.**

## INGREDIENTS

2¼ teaspoons active dry yeast
2 tablespoons sugar, divided
3 cups bread flour
1½ teaspoons salt
½ cup honey, divided
1 egg white, lightly beaten
3 tablespoons everything bagel seasoning

## METHOD

1. In a small bowl, combine 1 cup warm water (about 110°F/45°C), with the yeast and 1 tablespoon of the sugar. Stir gently and allow the mixture to rest at room temperature for 5 to 10 minutes, or until frothy.
2. In a large bowl, combine the bread flour, salt, and remaining 1 tablespoon of sugar. Make a well in the center and pour in the yeast mixture and half of the honey. Stir until a shaggy dough forms.
3. Turn the dough out onto a lightly floured surface and knead for about 8 to 10 minutes, or until the dough is smooth and elastic.

TRY THIS!

4. Divide the dough into 10 equal portions. Roll each portion into a ball, then use your thumb to poke a hole through the center. Gently stretch the dough outward to form a bagel shape, making sure the hole in the center is about 2 inches (5 cm) in diameter. They should be about 1 inch (2.5 cm) thick.
5. Place the shaped bagels on a baking sheet lined with parchment paper. Cover with a clean tea towel and let the bagels rise for 30 to 45 minutes, or until slightly puffy.
6. Preheat the oven to 425°F (220°C).
7. Meanwhile, bring a large pot of water to a boil over high heat, and whisk in the remaining ¼ cup of honey until fully dissolved.
8. Boil 2 to 3 bagels at a time. Cook for about 30 seconds on each side, then use a slotted spoon to transfer them back to the prepared baking sheet. Repeat until all bagels are cooked.
9. Brush the boiled bagels with the beaten egg white, then sprinkle generously with everything bagel seasoning.
10. Bake for 15 to 20 minutes, or until golden brown and cooked through.
11. Allow the bagels to cool on a wire rack for a few minutes before serving. Enjoy them warm with your favorite toppings!

# RAPPETIZERS

# SUMMERY-ASS WATERMELON + FETA SKEWERS

## with Mint Pesto

Serves 12 • Prep Time: 10 minutes • Cook Time: 1 minute • Total Time: 11 minutes

Kick off summer with these Watermelon Skewers! Juicy watermelon, tangy feta, and fresh mint pesto come together in a flavor explosion that's as refreshing as it is delicious. Perfect for picnics, barbecues, or any warm-weather gathering, these skewers are easy to make and a total crowd-pleaser. Just skewer, drizzle, and serve up some summer on a stick.

### INGREDIENTS

- 36 (1-inch [2.5 cm]) watermelon cubes
- 2× 8-ounce (226g) blocks of feta cheese, cut into 24 (½-inch [1.3 cm]) cubes
- 2 cups fresh mint leaves (packed)
- 1 cup flat-leaf parsley
- 1 garlic clove
- Pinch of black pepper
- Pinch of kosher salt
- ¼ cup olive oil
- ⅓ cup pine nuts
- ½ cup grated Parmesan
- 2 tablespoons balsamic glaze

#### SPECIAL EQUIPMENT

- 12 wooden skewers
- Food processor

### METHOD

1. Place 3 pieces of watermelon and 2 pieces of cheese on the skewers, alternating between the watermelon and cheese.
2. Bring 6 cups of water to a boil in a big ass pot. Fill a medium bowl with ice water and set it near the saucepan. Turn off the heat and add the mint and parsley to the pot. After 5 to 10 seconds, use a slotted spoon to transfer the herbs to the prepared ice bath. Gently swirl for 20 to 30 seconds (this will help the herbs keep their bright green color).
3. Strain the herbs with a fine mesh sieve and gently squeeze as much liquid out as humanly possible (alternatively, use a salad spinner).
4. Add the herbs, garlic, pepper, salt, half of the olive oil, pine nuts, and Parmesan to a food processor and pulse that shit until it's chopped. Then set to continuous speed and puree until smooth, while slowly drizzling in the remaining olive oil to create a silky emulsion.
5. Now go ahead and drizzle those skewers with your favorite balsamic glaze and serve pesto on the side as a dip or spoon on top of skewers.

# CORNY-ASS FRITTERS

Makes 12 fritters • Prep Time: 5 minutes • Cook Time: 12 minutes • Total Time: 17 minutes

**One sweltering afternoon in Savannah, Georgia, I was helping my friend James harvest some heirloom corn on his family farm. By the end of the day, I had worked up an appetite so big, I was ready to rip a husk off one of those cobs and eat that shit raw. But James was like, "Hold up, peanut! Let me whip you up some of my family's famous corn fritters." And boy, did he deliver. Those fritters were so crispy and divine, I almost considered asking James if I could be adopted into the family. But after researching and finding out how much paperwork is involved, I figured, I should just make 'em myself. So here they are: fritters so southern and corny, you'll feel like you're in a Nicholas Sparks novel. Enjoy.**

## INGREDIENTS

3 cups fresh or frozen corn (thawed and drained if using frozen)
1 cup all-purpose flour
1½ teaspoons granulated sugar
1 teaspoon baking powder
½ teaspoon black pepper
Pinch of kosher salt
2 large eggs
¾ cup whole milk
1 green onion, thinly sliced, plus more for topping
2 tablespoons vegetable oil

## METHOD

1 In a big-ass bowl, stir together the corn, flour, sugar, baking powder, pepper, and salt.

2 Add the eggs and milk and gently stir until a batter forms. Stir in the green onions.

3 Heat a large nonstick skillet over medium heat. Add the oil and swirl to coat. Once glistening, spoon 2 tablespoons of the corn mixture into the skillet and use the back of the spoon to flatten the mixture into a 3-inch (7.5 cm) wide disc.

4 Cook for 2 to 3 minutes per side or until golden and crispy.

5 Repeat, cooking 3 to 4 fritters per batch, until you've used all of your mixture.

6 Sprinkle with green onions and serve with Cheetah's secret spicy crème fraîche dipping sauce (recipe below).

## CHEETAH'S SECRET

CHEETAH'S SECRET SPICY CRÈME FRAÎCHE DIPPING SAUCE: IN A MEDIUM BOWL, WHISK TOGETHER 1 CUP CRÈME FRAÎCHE AND 3 TABLESPOONS (OR MORE!) OF YOUR FAVORITE HOT SAUCE (EXTRA POINTS IF IT HAS SOME SMOKINESS TO IT). STIR IN A DRIZZLE OF HONEY AND SERVE.

# MEDITERRANEAN-ASS NACHOS

Serves 4 • Prep Time: 5 minutes • Cook Time: 10-20 minutes • Total Time: 15-25 minutes

Say goodbye to regular, boring-ass nachos and wussup to a vibrant twist on a classic favorite. Inspired by a one-night stand I had in Mykonos with Elena, a local island chef with a body as perfect as the sunset over Santorini, these bad boys are piled high with crispy pita chips, creamy hummus, onions, olives, tomatoes, and a sprinkle of fresh herbs. It's like a Mediterranean feast in every bite, delivering a flavor punch that'll have you dreaming of sunny shores and crystal-clear waters, or in my case, my sweet, sweet Elena...

## INGREDIENTS

### CHEETAH'S HUMMUS

1½ cups cooked chickpeas, drained and rinsed
⅓ cup tahini
2 tablespoons olive oil
Juice of 1 lemon
1 garlic clove
Pinch of sea salt

### NACHOS

2 red bell peppers
1× 16-ounce (454g) bag pita chips
1 medium red onion, diced
1 beefsteak tomato, diced
1× 6.5-ounce (184g) can sliced olives
Fresh flat-leaf parsley leaves
Fresh mint leaves, roughly torn
Lemon zest

### SPECIAL EQUIPMENT

Blender or food processor

***Note:*** *If you do not own a gas grill, use a dry pan and cook the peppers on high heat until the skin blackens and blisters.*

## METHOD

1 Make the hummus: Place the chickpeas, tahini, olive oil, lemon juice, garlic, and salt in a blender or food processor. Blend until silky smooth. If the mixture is too thick, add water one tablespoon at a time until desired consistency.

2 If you have a gas stove, set the heat to medium-high. Add the peppers directly to the stovetop and cook, rotating often, until evenly charred on all sides. This can take anywhere from 10 to 20 minutes, depending on the size of the pepper and the heat of the stove. Trust your instincts (see Note)!

3 Allow the peppers to cool for 5 minutes. Roughly chop the pepper and remove any seeds.

4 Next is where the magic happens: building your nachos! Spread your pita chips on a serving tray or plate, spoon the hummus over them evenly, and sprinkle with pepper slices, onion, tomatoes, and olives. Throw down some parsley and mint. Sprinkle on the lemon zest and enjoy!

## CHEETAH'S SECRET

IF YOU WANT TO TAKE IT UP A NOTCH, MAKE THESE ZA'ATAR PITA CHIPS INSTEAD OF USING BAGGED ONES.

### ZA'ATAR PITA CHIPS

4 pita breads
¼ cup olive oil
3 tablespoons za'atar
Salt, to taste

1 Preheat the oven to 375°F (190°C).

2 Cut each pita bread into 8 wedges, then arrange the wedges on a baking sheet. Brush each wedge with olive oil using a pastry brush. Sprinkle the wedges with za'atar and salt.

3 Bake for 10 to 12 minutes, or until the pita chips are hot to the touch, golden brown and crispy. Check on those chips often so they don't burn!

# CHEETAH'S SECRET

**MAKE SOME BOMB-ASS, ZESTY-ASS PICKLED CHILI PEPPERS AHEAD OF TIME TO SPRINKLE ON TOP FOR A NICE POP OF COLOR AND KICK OF HEAT.**

¼ pound (113g) fresh chili peppers such as jalapeños or serranos, cut into ¼ inch (½ cm) rings
½ cup white vinegar
½ tablespoon sugar
¾ teaspoon salt
½ garlic clove, peeled and smashed
¼ teaspoon whole black peppercorns
¼ teaspoon mustard seeds (optional)
¼ bay leaf (optional)

1 In a small saucepan over high heat, combine the vinegar, ¼ cup water, sugar, salt, garlic, peppercorns, mustard seeds and bay leaf (if using). Bring to a boil, stirring occasionally.

2 In the meantime, arrange the sliced chili peppers in a clean, sterilized jar.

3 Carefully pour the hot brine over the peppers, making sure the peppers are completely submerged. Use a spoon to press the peppers down if needed.

4 Place the lid on the jar and let it cool to room temperature. Once cooled, transfer to the refrigerator.

5 Allow the peppers to pickle for at least 24 hours before eating for optimal flavor. They're gonna continue to develop flavor over the next few days and will be good for about 2 to 3 weeks. Enjoy over your cauliflower bites or anything you'd like to have a little kick and color!

# ZESTY-ASS ZA'ATAR CAULIFLOWER BITES

## with Tahini Dip

Serves 4 • Prep Time: 6 minutes • Cook Time: 13 minutes • Total Time: 19 minutes

These succulent bites of cauliflower are roasted to perfection, seasoned with a heavy dose of Middle Eastern flavor, then taken to the next level with a creamy, rich, and zingy tahini dip. Perfect for parties, gatherings, or any occasion where you want to impress without the stress, these bites are ridiculously easy to make. Roast, dip, and watch them disappear. If Noah's around, keep an eye out, because they won't even make it to the table before they're gone, and you'll have to make another batch for the rest of your guests. Luckily, they're so simple to make that you can just whip up some more.

### INGREDIENTS

1 cup panko breadcrumbs
3½ teaspoons za'atar
Pinch of kosher salt
1 large egg, beaten
2 cups cauliflower florets
2 garlic cloves, grated
½ cup tahini
3 tablespoons fresh lemon juice
Lemon wedges, for serving

#### SPECIAL EQUIPMENT

Air fryer

### METHOD

1. Preheat an air fryer to 375°F (190°C).
2. In a shallow bowl, stir together the breadcrumbs, za'atar, and salt.
3. Add the egg to another shallow bowl.
4. Dip the cauliflower into the egg, then add it to the breadcrumb mixture and toss that shit around until it's fully coated. Gently press the bread crumbs into the cauliflower. Transfer to an air fryer basket and cook for 9 to 13 minutes until golden and soft enough to be pierced by a fork. You may need to work in batches.
5. Meanwhile, in a medium bowl, whisk together the garlic, tahini, and lemon juice. Add water as needed to reach your desired consistency.
6. Serve the cauliflower with the tahini sauce (for dipping) and lemon wedges on the side.

# SMOKY-ASS SALMON DIP

## with Everything Bagel Chips

Serves 10 • Prep Time: 10 minutes • Cook Time: 10 minutes • Total Time: 20 minutes

Have you ever reached for a bagel only to find it was stale? Well, sometimes a minor disappointment is a blessing in disguise. So don't miss out on that bread. Instead, turn them into crunchy, savory everything bagel chips. They're impossible not to love. Add a delicious, easy dip (just toss everything into a food processor and process that shit) and whether you're hosting a casual get-together or an elegant brunch, everyone will be coming back for seconds (and maybe even thirds). So, go ahead and serve up some of my Smoky-Ass Salmon Dip, and watch your brunch go from zero to hero in one delicious scoop.

### INGREDIENTS

#### FOR THE BAGEL CHIPS

5 bagels

Olive oil

Everything bagel seasoning, to taste

#### FOR THE DIP

1 block (8 ounces [227g]) cream cheese, softened

¼ cup Greek yogurt (any fat percentage)

¼ cup mayonnaise (optional)

1 tablespoon fresh lemon juice

2 tablespoons capers, drained

2 tablespoons minced red onion

3 tablespoons chopped fresh dill, plus more for garnish

4 ounces (113g) lox, roughly chopped

Kosher salt, to taste

#### SPECIAL EQUIPMENT:

Food processor or blender

### METHOD

#### FOR THE BAGEL CHIPS

1. Preheat the oven to 375°F (190°C).
2. Cut bagels in half then slice 'em as thin as you can—⅛ to ¼-inch (3mm to ½ cm) thick is what you're looking for.
3. Arrange the bagel slices on a baking sheet and brush with olive oil.
4. Generously sprinkle with everything bagel seasoning.
5. Bake for 10 minutes or until golden, checking often to prevent burning.
6. Allow the bagels to cool slightly before transferring to a cooling rack.
7. Enjoy immediately or store in an airtight container for up to 2 weeks.

#### FOR THE SALMON DIP

1. Place cream cheese, Greek yogurt, mayonnaise, lemon juice, capers, onion, dill, lox, and salt into a food processor or blender and blitz until well mixed and creamy. Scrape down the sides of the food processor, if necessary. Transfer to a serving bowl, garnish with dill, and serve with bagel chips.

# CRABBY-ASS CAKES

Makes **6-7 big ass cakes** • Prep Time: **5 minutes** • Cook Time: **15 minutes** • Total Time: **20 minutes**

Get ready to dive into a sea of flavor with these delicious crab cakes that make all other crab cakes seem like crap cakes. These beauties are packed with juicy, tender crab meat, just the right amount of seasoning, and a touch of magic that'll have you hooked from the first bite. Crispy on the outside, moist and flavorful on the inside, they're like a seafood dream come true. They're perfect for a brunch party or as a starter to an evening meal. Either way, whoever eats these will be extremely impressed, even if it's just you.

## INGREDIENTS

### CRAB CAKES

1 pound (454g) fresh lump crab meat
⅔ cup bread crumbs
¼ cup mayonnaise
1 large egg
1 tablespoon fresh flat-leaf parsley leaves, chopped
2 teaspoons Worcestershire sauce
1½ teaspoons yellow mustard
1 teaspoon black pepper
¾ teaspoon onion powder
Pinch of kosher salt
Louisiana-style hot sauce, to taste
3 tablespoons unsalted butter

### TARTAR SAUCE

1 cup mayonnaise
¼ cup chopped pickles
2 tablespoons fresh lemon juice
1 tablespoon minced fresh dill
Pepper, to taste

## METHOD

1. In a medium bowl, mix together the crab meat, bread crumbs, mayonnaise, egg, parsley, Worcestershire sauce, mustard, pepper, onion powder, salt, and hot sauce. Mix it real good.
2. Use your hands to form the mixture into 3-inch (7.5cm) wide patties, about 1.5-inch (4cm) thick.
3. Heat a large skillet over medium heat and add 1 tablespoon of butter. Cook 3 to 4 of those muthafuckas (depending on the size of your skillet) for 3 to 5 minutes on each side until golden. Transfer to a serving platter. Repeat with the remaining patties, cooking in batches.
4. In a small bowl, whisk together the mayonnaise, pickles, lemon juice, dill, and pepper. Whisk until that shit is smoother than your mama's silk sheets. Add the sauce to the platter and serve.

## CHEETAH'S SECRET

TAKE THESE CRAB CAKES UP A NOTCH BY SLAPPING THEM ON SOME TOASTED HAWAIIAN-STYLE DINNER ROLLS SLATHERED WITH TARTAR SAUCE. MAKE SURE YOU TOAST THOSE BUNS, THOUGH. NOBODY LIKES A SOGGY BOTTOM.

# TASTY-ASS BACON-WRAPPED DATES

Serves 6 (makes 24 dates) • Prep Time: 10 minutes • Cook Time: 25 minutes • Total Time: 35 minutes

**These tasty bite-sized treats will have you shouting, *"Good lord, these are some tasty bite-sized treats!"* This is a sure-fire way to ensure that your dinner party guests finally think you're not a failure. Serve them up, watch them disappear, and get ready for the inevitable requests for the recipe.**

## INGREDIENTS

24 large Medjool dates, pitted

4 ounces (38g) crumbled goat cheese

¼ cup honey or maple syrup

¼ cup walnuts, chopped

12 slices thin applewood smoked bacon, cut in half crosswise

## METHOD

1. Preheat the oven to 375°F (190°C) and line a baking sheet with parchment paper.
2. Slice into each date lengthwise to create a pocket. Take care not to cut them all the way through.
3. In a small bowl, mix the goat cheese, honey, and walnuts until combined.
4. Spoon about ½ teaspoon (or as much as you can stuff in without it spilling out) of the goat cheese mixture into each date and then use your fingers to lightly pinch the stuffed date closed.
5. Place 1 date at the end of a bacon half and roll until the date is fully wrapped. Secure with a toothpick and transfer to the prepared baking sheet, leaving 1 inch (2.5 cm) of space between each.
6. Bake for 18 to 22 minutes or until bacon is fully cooked.
7. Let cool for 2 to 3 minutes and enjoy!

## CHEETAH'S SECRET

YOU CAN ADD ANY SOFT CHEESE YOU LIKE TO THE DATES. IF YOU'RE INTO BLUE CHEESE, FEEL FREE TO USE IT INSTEAD OF GOAT CHEESE. SOMETIMES I EVEN THROW DOWN WITH SOME WHIPPED FETA.

# HOT-ASS AIR FRYER WINGS

Serves **4** • Prep Time: **5 minutes** • Cook Time: **9 minutes** • Total Time: **14 minutes**

**Brace yourself for the crispiest, juiciest air-fried wings to ever come out of the Goodboy's House kitchen. These bad boys are not your average wings—they've got a secret weapon: baking soda. That's right, this magical ingredient makes the skin so crispy, you'll think they've been deep-fried. This little trick is a gem I picked up on my travels, and now I'm sharing it with you so you can get the perfect wings without the hassle and unwanted calories of deep frying. Perfect for game day, impressing friends, or just treating yourself to something delicious, these'll have you licking your fingers and begging for more.**

## INGREDIENTS

2 pounds (907g) chicken wings
2 tablespoons salted butter, melted and cooled
1 teaspoon kosher salt
1 teaspoon garlic powder
1 teaspoon onion powder
1 teaspoon paprika (sweet or smoked)
1 teaspoon chili powder
Black pepper, to taste
1 tablespoon baking powder
2 tablespoons cornstarch
Hot honey, for serving
Sesame seeds, for serving
Chopped scallions, for serving

### SPECIAL EQUIPMENT

Air fryer

## METHOD

1. Preheat the air fryer to 400°F (200°C) for 5 minutes.
2. Meanwhile, pat the chicken completely dry with paper towels.
3. Combine all of the spices plus the baking powder and cornstarch in a bowl to make your wing rub.
4. In a big-ass bowl, toss the wings with the rub mixture until completely coated.
5. Arrange the wings in the air fryer basket in a single layer, being careful not to overcrowd. You may need to work in batches. Cook until crispy and cooked through, about 7 to 9 minutes. The internal temperature should be 165°F (74°C) and the wings should be golden brown in color.
6. Drizzle with hot honey or sprinkle with sesame seeds and scallions and serve with any sauce you like.

## CHEETAH'S SECRET

FOR AN EXOTIC TWIST ON BUFFALO WINGS, MAKE MY CURRY BUFFALO SAUCE: MELT 5 TABLESPOONS OF BUTTER IN A SMALL SAUCEPAN OVER MEDIUM-LOW HEAT. STIR IN 1 TABLESPOON OF CURRY POWDER. ADD 4 TABLESPOONS OF YOUR FAVORITE HOT SAUCE AND COOK 2 TO 3 MINUTES MORE, UNTIL BUBBLING. COAT YOUR COOKED WINGS WITH THE SAUCE AND ENJOY, BUT BEWARE: YOU MAY NEVER GO BACK TO REGULAR BUFFALO WINGS AGAIN.

# COUNTRY-ASS BBQ CHICKEN MINI SLIDERS

## with a Quick Pickle

Serves 10-12 • Prep Time: 15 minutes • Cook Time: 4 hours • Total Time: 4 hours 15 minutes

**Get ready to take your pie hole on a down-home flavor trip with these Pulled BBQ Chicken Mini Sliders. Tender, juicy pulled chicken smothered in smoky, tangy BBQ sauce, piled onto fluffy mini buns, and finished with zingy homemade pickles. They say everything is bigger in Texas...but not these little muthafuckas!**

### INGREDIENTS

#### PICKLES

1 cucumber, peeled and thinly sliced

1 cup white vinegar

2 tablespoons granulated sugar

1 teaspoon kosher salt

½ teaspoon whole black peppercorns

#### CHICKEN

1× 18-ounce (510g) bottle sweet barbecue sauce

¼ cup apple cider vinegar

2 pounds (907g) boneless, skinless chicken breasts

2 pounds (907g) boneless, skinless chicken thighs

Kosher salt and black pepper

1 medium white onion, thinly sliced

#### TO ASSEMBLE

6 tablespoons butter

1× (24-count) package Hawaiian-style slider rolls

#### SPECIAL EQUIPMENT

Slow cooker

### METHOD

1. Make the pickles: In a small container with a lid, add 2 cups of water and the vinegar. Add the sugar and salt and stir to dissolve. Add the peppercorns, then the cucumber slices and cover tightly with a lid. Refrigerate for at least 30 minutes before using.
2. Next, make the chicken: In a large bowl, whisk together the barbecue sauce, vinegar, and ½ cup water.
3. Season the chicken breasts and thighs all over with salt and pepper. Place the chicken in a slow cooker. Add the onion and pour in the barbecue sauce-vinegar mixture. Cover and cook on high for 3½ hours.
4. Shred the chicken using two forks. Return the chicken to the slow cooker and toss with the juices. Cut the heat.
5. To assemble, butter both sides of a dinner roll and toast on a skillet set over medium heat until golden brown. Pile on a serving of shredded chicken to the bottom of the roll. Top with pickles. Close the sandwich and serve. Repeat with remaining ingredients until the chicken and rolls are gone like your money after tax season.

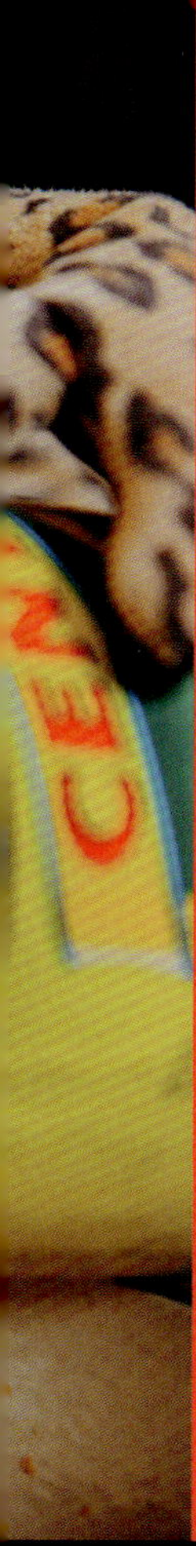

WASSOUP!

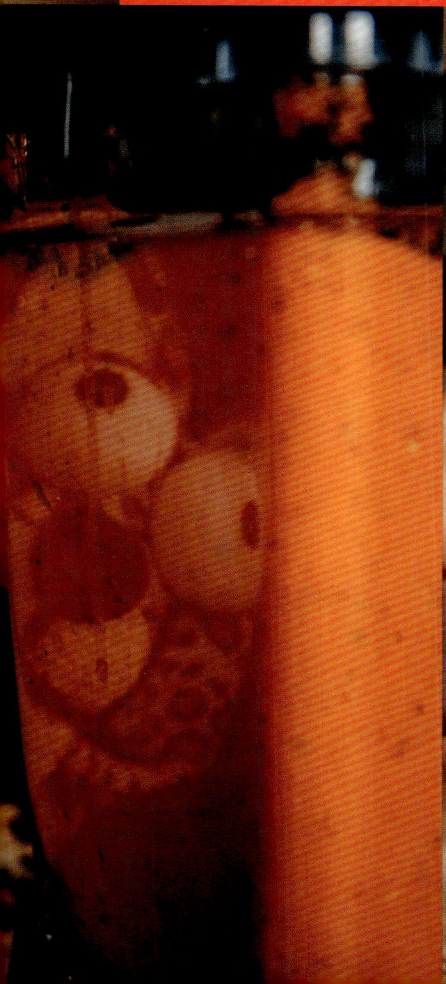

# LUSCIOUS-ASS TOMATO SOUP

Serves 6 • Prep Time: 5 minutes • Cook Time: 1 hour 15 minutes • Total Time: 1 hour 20 minutes

This isn't your average tomato soup; this tomato soup is a rich, velvety potion that's been simmered to perfection and seasoned with just the right amount of pizzazz. Perfect for cozy nights, quick lunches, or impressing guests, this soup is as easy to make as it is to devour. Roast, blend, season, and serve—simple as that. It's the kind of soup that turns a humble tomato into a gourmet experience.

## INGREDIENTS

- 8 tablespoons butter
- 1 large white onion, roughly chopped
- 2× 28-ounce (794g) cans crushed tomatoes
- 4 cups chicken broth
- 6 garlic cloves, minced
- 2 teaspoons kosher salt
- 1 teaspoon dried oregano
- 1 tablespoon smoked paprika
- 1 teaspoon dried basil
- ¾ cup heavy cream
- 1 cup crème fraîche
- 12 fresh basil leaves
- 6 tablespoons olive oil

### SPECIAL EQUIPMENT

Blender or immersion blender

## METHOD

1. In a big ass pot, melt the butter over medium-low heat. Add the onion, crushed tomatoes, chicken broth, garlic, salt, oregano, smoked paprika, and dried basil.
2. Bring to a boil over medium-high heat. Reduce heat to low and allow to simmer, uncovered, for 35 minutes. Stir frequently to make sure nothing sticks.
3. Turn off the heat and allow the soup to cool for 10 or so minutes, then transfer it to the base of a blender. Blend on low for 1 to 2 minutes. Increase the speed to high and blend for 1 to 2 more minutes until the soup is smooth and no chunks remain.
4. Carefully pour the soup back into the pot and stir in the heavy cream. Simmer on low for 10 more minutes.
5. Divide between 12 bowls and top with a dollop of crème fraîche, a basil leaf, and 1 tablespoon of drizzled olive oil.

## CHEETAH'S SECRET

SERVE YOUR TOMATO SOUP WITH SOME CHEESY CROSTINI: PREHEAT THE OVEN TO 350°F (175°C). LINE A BAKING SHEET WITH PARCHMENT PAPER. CUT A BAGUETTE INTO 1-INCH (2CM) SLICES ON A BIAS AND PLACE THEM ON THE PREPARED BAKING SHEET. DRIZZLE WITH OLIVE OIL, THEN SPRINKLE WITH FRESHLY GRATED PARMESAN AND DRIED OREGANO. BAKE FOR 10 MINUTES OR UNTIL GOLDEN.

# CREAMY-ASS BUTTERNUT SQUASH SOUP

Serves 6 • Prep Time: 8 minutes • Cook Time: 1 hour 10 minutes • Total Time: 1 hour 18 minutes

**Grab a spoon and get ready for a soup that's creamy, velvety, and downright irresistible. It's the perfect soup for autumn with its deep flavors. It's the kind of soup that makes you feel all warm and fuzzy inside, even if the weather outside is less than inviting. Make it for your significant other if you wanna stay real warm in bed tonight, if you know what I mean.**

## INGREDIENTS

1 large butternut squash, cut in half lengthwise
1 tablespoon olive oil
2 garlic cloves, sliced
1 medium shallot, diced
1 tablespoon minced fresh ginger
1 tablespoon ground turmeric
½ tablespoon ground coriander
1 tablespoon kosher salt, plus more for seasoning
1 tablespoon black pepper, plus more for seasoning
3 cups vegetable broth
½ cup coconut milk
Heavy cream or olive oil, for drizzling
Chopped fresh parsley leaves, for garnish
Roasted pumpkin seeds (pepitas), for garnish

### SPECIAL EQUIPMENT

Immersion blender or blender

## METHOD

1. Preheat the oven to 400°F (200°F).
2. Use a spoon to remove the seeds and "guts" from the squash.
3. Line a baking sheet with parchment paper and place your squash cut-side down.
4. Bake for 1 hour.
5. Remove from the oven and let cool for 5 minutes.
6. Scoop the flesh out and transfer it to a medium bowl.
7. Heat a big ass pot over medium heat. Add the olive oil. Once glistening, add the garlic, shallot, ginger, and turmeric. Cook until fragrant and translucent, about 3 to 5 minutes.
8. Throw in the coriander, salt, and pepper, and cook for an additional minute.
9. Add the vegetable broth, coconut milk, and ½ cup water. Stir. Add the squash and stir again. Bring to a boil over high heat, then reduce the heat to medium and simmer for 2 minutes. Turn off heat.
10. Using an immersion blender, blend until smooth (see Note).
11. Add more salt and pepper, if needed.
12. Garnish with a drizzle of heavy cream or olive oil, top with parsley and pumpkin seeds, and enjoy.

***Note:*** *If you don't own an immersion blender, don't stress! You can use a regular blender. Just allow the soup to cool for 10 or so minutes, transfer to the base of a blender, and process that shit on low (your soup, not your feelings) for 1 to 2 minutes. Once everything is homogenous, increase the speed to high and blend for 1 to 2 more minutes, until the soup is smooth and creamy as... you can fill in the blank here, nasty-ass.*

# EASY-ASS EGG DROP SOUP

Serves 6 • Prep Time: 6 minutes • Cook Time: 20 minutes • Total Time: 26 minutes

**Neih-hou, muthafuckas! Get ready to whip up one of my all-time favorite soups—a dish that's so simple, you'll wonder why you ever ordered the takeout version. With silky egg ribbons swirling in a savory, velvety broth, this classic Chinese soup is a breeze to make. Even Noah made it one night, and he's dumb as hell.**

## INGREDIENTS

6 cups chicken broth
1 tablespoon minced fresh ginger
1 tablespoon garlic powder
½ tablespoon black pepper
⅓ tablespoon sugar
2 tablespoons soy sauce
Dash ground turmeric
1 tablespoon sesame oil
1 tablespoon cornstarch
2 large eggs, beaten
1 scallion, chopped

## METHOD

1 Pour the chicken broth into a big ass pot set over medium-high heat. Throw in the ginger, garlic, pepper, sugar, soy sauce, turmeric, and sesame oil.

2 Make the slurry by whisking together the cornstarch and 1 tablespoon cold water in a small bowl until there are no lumps. Slowly whisk into the soup. Allow the soup to simmer for 10 minutes.

3 While stirring, slowly add the egg bit by bit.

4 Gently stir in the scallion. Turn off the heat and serve.

TRY THIS!

# FANCY-ASS INSTANT RAMEN

Serves 1 • Prep Time: 6 minutes • Cook Time: 10 minutes • Total Time: 16 minutes

Who says instant ramen has to be boring and basic? Elevate your noodle game with this Fancy-Ass Instant Ramen—a dish that takes your favorite budget-friendly staple and transforms it into a gourmet masterpiece. So when you're in a hurry, there's no need to worry. All it takes is a few simple upgrades, and you'll go from college dorm cuisine to a Michelin-worthy bowl.

## INGREDIENTS

1 × 3-ounce (85g) package ramen
1 large egg
½ teaspoon chili oil
1 garlic clove, minced
1 tablespoon dark soy sauce
2 tablespoons kimchi
4 tablespoons assorted fresh vegetables such as sliced radishes and mushrooms
1 scallion, thinly sliced
Sesame seeds, for topping

## METHOD

1. Cook the ramen according to the package instructions, but throw away the flavor packet. We're gonna be adding our own flavor. When it's done, drain that shit.
2. Meanwhile, fill a small bowl with cold water. Bring a small pot of water to a boil. Carefully add the egg and cook for about 7 minutes for a soft-boiled egg or adjust to your preferred doneness. Use a slotted spoon to transfer the cooked egg to the prepared bowl (to stop the cooking process). Peel the egg and set aside.
3. Add the cooked ramen noodles to a bowl. Pour in the chili oil, garlic, and dark soy sauce. Toss to coat. Add the kimchi and vegetables.
4. Carefully slice the soft-boiled egg in half lengthwise and place it on top of the noodles.
5. Sprinkle with sliced scallions and sesame seeds and serve!

## CHEETAH'S SECRET

ADD YOUR OWN GARLIC CHILI CRUNCH (RECIPE BELOW) ON TOP FOR AN EVEN BIGGER FLAVOR PUNCH.

### GARLIC CHILI CRUNCH

1 cup vegetable oil (or any neutral oil)
6 garlic cloves, minced
¼ cup crushed red pepper flakes
1 tablespoon soy sauce
1 tablespoon sugar
1 teaspoon salt

1. In a small saucepan, heat the vegetable oil over medium heat until it shimmers. Add the garlic, reduce the heat to low and cook, stirring frequently, until the garlic turns golden brown and crispy. Be careful not to burn the garlic.
2. Once the garlic is golden, remove the saucepan from the heat.
3. Add the red pepper flakes and stir well.
4. Stir in the soy sauce, sugar, and salt to the mixture.
5. Allow the Garlic Chili Crunch to cool completely in the saucepan.
6. Once cooled, transfer it to an airtight container.
7. Enjoy now or store the Garlic Chili Crunch in the refrigerator for up to a month!

# BUBBE'S YIDDISH-ASS MATZO BALL SOUP

Serves 6 • Prep Time: 6 minutes • Cook Time: 1 hour 30 minutes • Total Time: 1 hour 36 minutes

**Welcome to Matzo Ball Soup 101, with a recipe that's so good, it should come with a warning: May cause uncontrollable nostalgia and family feuds over who gets to eat the last juicy ball. Look at these fluffy matzo balls bobbing in that savory, mouth-watering chicken broth. It's the kind of soup that can cure a cold, mend a broken heart, and provide a brief distraction from decades of unaddressed family tension.**

## INGREDIENTS

### FOR THE SOUP

1 tablespoon vegetable oil
3 celery stalks, chopped
1 medium white onion, chopped
3 carrots, peeled and chopped
6 cups chicken stock
1 whole chicken, rinsed and patted dry
1 tablespoon fresh flat-leaf parsley, chopped
3 bay leaves
1 tablespoon chopped fresh dill

### FOR THE MATZO BALLS

4 large eggs
¼ cup schmaltz (see Note)
1 cup matzo meal
1 teaspoon baking powder
1 tablespoon garlic powder
1 tablespoon onion powder
1½ teaspoons kosher salt
1 tablespoon black pepper

## METHOD

1. Heat a big ass stock pot over high heat for 3 minutes.
2. Add 1 tablespoon of oil, then add the celery, onion, and carrots. Cook for 3 to 5 minutes, until the vegetables begin to soften.
3. Add 6 cups of water and the chicken stock, and bring that shit to a boil.
4. Throw in the chicken, parsley, bay leaves, and dill. Cook over medium-high heat for 30 to 40 minutes. Remove the bay leaf when it's done simmering.
5. Meanwhile, mix the eggs and schmaltz in a medium bowl.
6. In a large bowl, stir together the matzo meal, baking powder, garlic powder, onion powder, salt, and pepper.
7. Stir the wet ingredients into the dry ingredients and mix until fully combined.
8. Roll mixture into uniform 2-inch (5cm) balls.
9. Bring a large pot of water to a simmer over medium heat. Drop the balls into the pot, cover, and cook for 20 to 30 minutes or until the balls look fluffy and are floating.
10. Place 1 ball into each bowl and cover with soup. Enjoy!

***Note:** Now you may be wondering what in the hell "Schmaltz" is. I was once like you, uninformed in the subtleties of Ashkenazi jewish cooking, until my friend Rabbi Yoni explained that Schmaltz is just the yiddish word for "Chicken Fat". If you don't have access to this matzo-ball cheat code, don't fret! Just substitute with any oil or even melted butter, and you'll still have a deliciously fluffy ball.*

# TANGY-ASS LEMON CHICKEN RICE SOUP

Serves 6 • Prep Time: 5 minutes • Cook Time: 4 hours • Total Time: 4 hours 5 minutes

**This soup is inspired by my trip to the Island of Crete where I made sweet love to Athena, a local chicken farmer's wife. It combines tender chicken, fluffy rice, and a refreshing splash of lemon, delivering a flavor experience that's both tangy and satisfying. Serve up a bowl of zesty comfort guaranteed to brighten up any dark day like a burst of Greek sunshine.**

## INGREDIENTS

3 tablespoons olive oil
1 cup diced carrots
1 large onion, diced
4 celery stalks, diced
3 teaspoons minced garlic
Zest of 1 lemon
3 skin-on, bone-in chicken leg quarters
6 cups unsalted chicken broth
6 tablespoons fresh lemon juice
1 cup arborio rice
Lemon wedges, for serving
Black pepper, to taste
Salt, to taste
Chopped fresh parsley, for garnish

## METHOD

1. Heat the oil in a big ass pot over medium heat. Add the carrots, onion, and celery. Cook for 3 minutes, stirring occasionally.
2. Add the garlic and lemon zest and cook for 30 seconds. Set the chicken legs on top of the vegetables.
3. Add the broth and bring to a boil over high heat, stirring occasionally.
4. Reduce to medium-low, cover, and simmer for 3 hours, stirring every 20 to 30 minutes.
5. Remove the chicken and set aside. Allow the broth to simmer for 20 more minutes.
6. Remove the skin, bones, and any cartilage from the chicken and discard. Shred the remaining meat with two forks. Stir the shredded chicken into the soup. Add the lemon juice, then the rice, stir, and cook uncovered until the rice is tender, about 30 minutes.
7. Serve in bowls with a squeeze of lemon, fresh black pepper, salt, and parsley.

# CHEETAH'S HEARTY-ASS CHILI

Serves **6** • Prep Time: **6 minutes** • Cook Time: **25 minutes** • Total Time: **31 minutes**

All right, check it out. If you're trying to bring the heat to your tailgate, then whip up this easy chili. It's as lean as a pro-bowl running back and so tasty it will have you doing a touchdown dance in the parking lot. Packed with succulent meat, hearty beans, and a plethora of spices, this dish is the ultimate crowd-pleaser. I made a version of this recipe when I was tailgating at the Michigan vs. Ohio State game awhile back. This chili had the Wolverines and Buckeye fans momentarily forgetting their differences as they devoured their bowls instead of each other.

## INGREDIENTS

- 2 teaspoons olive oil
- 1 pound (454g) ground turkey
- 1 large red or yellow onion, chopped
- 2 garlic cloves, minced
- 1 yellow bell pepper, seeded and chopped
- 2× 28-ounce (794g) cans diced tomatoes
- 2× 29-ounce (822g) cans tomato sauce
- 1× 15.5-ounce (439g) can kidney beans, rinsed and drained
- 1× 15.5-ounce (439g) can black beans, rinsed and drained
- 2 tablespoons chili powder
- 2 teaspoons cumin
- ½ teaspoon smoked paprika
- ½ teaspoon dried oregano
- 2 teaspoons kosher salt
- 1 teaspoon dark brown sugar
- Sour cream, shredded cheddar, or green onion, for serving (optional)

## METHOD

1. Heat a large pot over medium heat. Add the oil. Once glistening, add the turkey, onion, and garlic. Cook, stirring often, until the meat is browned, about 7 to 10 minutes.
2. Add the pepper and cook for 2 minutes.
3. Stir in the diced tomatoes, tomato sauce, kidney beans, black beans, chili powder, cumin, paprika, oregano, salt, and brown sugar.
4. Increase the heat to medium-high and bring to a boil.
5. Once that shit is boiling, reduce heat to medium-low and allow to simmer. Stir occasionally, for at least 15 minutes or up to 1 hour (if you have the time, this will allow the flavor to develop much more).
6. Ladle that delicious chili into bowls and serve with sour cream, cheese, and a sprinkle of green onion (if using).

## CHEETAH'S SECRET

LOOKING FOR A GAME-DAY APPETIZER? NO PROBLEM. TRY THESE CHILI POTATO SKINS: BAKE A RUSSET POTATO AT 400°F (200°C) FOR 45 MINUTES OR UNTIL TENDER. LET COOL SLIGHTLY, THEN CUT IN HALF AND SCOOP OUT THE INSIDE (DISCARD OR SAVE FOR ANOTHER PURPOSE). FILL THE POTATO, LAYERING WITH CHILI, SOUR CREAM, AND CHEDDAR CHEESE. BAKE FOR 5 MORE MINUTES. GARNISH WITH CHOPPED SCALLIONS AND DIG IN!

# SCRUMPTIOUS-ASS CURRY LENTIL SOUP

## with Spinach and Potato

Serves 6 • Prep Time: 10 minutes • Cook Time: 30 minutes • Total Time: 40 minutes

If you're looking for a recipe that will make your tastebuds do a muthafuckin' backflip, look no further. This curry is not only healthy, but also hearty thanks to lentils, potatoes, and spinach all swimming in a curry-based broth that's so good you'll want to take a bath in it. This easy soup will be as comforting as your favorite sweatpants, but way tastier.

### INGREDIENTS

3 tablespoons olive oil
½ large onion, chopped
2 garlic cloves, finely chopped
3 tablespoons red curry paste
6 medium potatoes, peeled and roughly chopped
4 carrots, peeled and chopped
4 cups vegetable broth
1 cup red lentils, washed and rinsed
1× 10-ounce (284g) package frozen chopped spinach, thawed
Salt and pepper, to taste

### METHOD

1. Fire up a big ass pot over high heat. Add the oil. Once shimmering, add the onion and make 'em sweat like a sinner in church until fragrant and translucent.
2. Add the garlic and curry paste, and cook, stirring constantly, for 45 seconds to 1 minute.
3. Add the potatoes and carrots and cook. Make sure to stir that shit up often, for 4 to 5 minutes.
4. Add the vegetable broth, lentils, and spinach. Stir to combine.
5. Boil for 2 to 3 minutes. Reduce the heat to low, cover, and cook until the potatoes are soft like butter, about 15 to 20 minutes. Season, to taste, with salt and pepper. Ladle into bowls and enjoy!

### CHEETAH'S SECRET

YOU CAN TURN THIS SOUP INTO A CURRY TO SERVE OVER RICE BY OMITTING THE VEGETABLE BROTH AND REPLACING IT WITH 1 (13.5-OUNCE (400ML)) CAN OF COCONUT MILK. I ALSO LIKE TO ADD 1 TEASPOON OF TURMERIC.

# THAT GOOD GREEN

# SMASHED-ASS CUCUMBER SALAD

## with Sesame Dressing

Serves 4 • Prep Time: 17 minutes • Cook Time: 20 minutes (marinating time) • Total Time: 37 minutes

When it comes to being simple, nobody does it better than Noah. I drew great inspiration from my curly-headed friend when coming up with this recipe. I kept it simple with just a few ingredients. All it takes is a quick smash, and plain cucumbers magically transform into a refreshing, mouthwatering dish. Tossed in a tangy dressing of soy sauce, rice vinegar, garlic, and a touch of spice, this salad is both cooling and zesty—perfect for any occasion. Smashing the cucumbers allows them to absorb more of the savory, tangy dressing, making each bite an absolute taste bud sensation. Enjoy the fresh, vibrant flavors and the satisfying crunch with this testament to how a few simple ingredients, when combined just right, can create something truly special. Just like Noah.

### INGREDIENTS

2 large English cucumbers
½ teaspoon salt
1 tablespoon soy sauce
1 tablespoon rice vinegar
1 tablespoon sesame oil
1 tablespoon granulated sugar
1 teaspoon minced garlic
1½ tablespoons toasted sesame seeds
2 spring onions (or scallions), thinly sliced
1 teaspoon crushed hot red pepper flakes (optional)

### METHOD

1. Cut the cucumbers in half lengthwise and place them cut-side down on a cutting board. Gently smash them with the flat side of a knife or a rolling pin until they crack and split. Cut into ½-inch (1 cm) pieces.
2. Place the cucumber pieces in a colander and sprinkle with the salt. Toss to coat evenly and let sit for 15 to 20 minutes to draw out excess water.
3. Meanwhile, in a small bowl, combine the soy sauce, rice vinegar, sesame oil, sugar, and minced garlic. Stir until the sugar is dissolved.
4. Pat the cucumbers dry with paper towels and transfer to a large bowl.
5. Pour the sesame oil mixture over the cucumbers and toss to coat evenly.
6. Sprinkle it with toasted sesame seeds and thinly sliced spring onions and give that shit a final toss.
7. Let it chill in the refrigerator for 10 to 15 minutes to allow the flavors to come together, then serve.

## CHEETAH'S SECRET

**FEEL FREE TO ADD ANY OTHER HERBS YOU LIKE. I LIKE TO ADD CHOPPED CILANTRO OR SOME PICKLED GINGER. HERE IS MY GO-TO RECIPE:**

### EASY PICKLED GINGER

1 cup fresh ginger, peeled and thinly sliced
½ cup rice vinegar
¼ cup granulated sugar
1 teaspoon salt

1 Bring a small pot of water to a boil. Add the sliced ginger to the boiling water and cook for 1 to 2 minutes. Drain and set aside.

2 Meanwhile, in another small pot, stir together the rice vinegar, sugar, salt, and ½ cup water. Heat over medium heat, stirring until the sugar and salt are completely dissolved. Remove from heat and let the mixture cool slightly.

3 Transfer the cooked ginger to a mason jar, cover with liquid, seal, and store in the refrigerator for up to 2 weeks.

# FRESH-ASS FENNEL SALAD

Serves 4 • Prep Time: 10 minutes • Cook Time: 40 minutes • Total Time: 50 minutes

**This salad is a breeze to assemble but looks and tastes like a million bucks. It's the kind of dish that makes you feel like you've got your life together, even if you're just trying to eat more veggies. With crisp, aromatic fennel mingling with sweet, roasted beets, creamy goat cheese, and crunchy toasted walnuts, you've got a salad that's sophisticated, scrum-diddly-umptious, and fresh as fuck.**

## INGREDIENTS

3 large beets, peeled and cut into 1-inch (2.5cm) pieces

2 tablespoons extra-virgin olive oil, plus more for topping

1 cup chopped walnuts

½ teaspoon salt, divided

½ teaspoon freshly ground black pepper

2 fennel bulbs with fronds, cored and thinly sliced

3 scallions, chopped

Juice of 1 medium lemon (about 2 tablespoons)

3 ounces crumbled goat cheese

## METHOD

1. Preheat the oven to 400°F (200°C).
2. Toss the beet pieces with olive oil and place in a single layer on a baking sheet. Roast until tender enough to be pierced by a knife, about 20 to 30 minutes.
3. Meanwhile, heat a medium pan over medium-low heat. Add the walnuts, ¼ teaspoon salt, and pepper and toast, stirring frequently, for 2 to 3 minutes or until the walnuts get toasty and fragrant. Keep an eye on these bad boys, they tend to burn easily!
4. To a large-ass serving bowl, add the fennel (including the fronds), scallions, beets, lemon juice and the remaining ¼ teaspoon salt. Toss that shit. The salad is going to turn nice and pink from the beets—that's when you know it's ready.
5. Sprinkle the walnuts over the top of the salad, top with the crumbled goat cheeze, drizzle with olive oil, and enjoy.

## CHEETAH'S SECRET

YOU CAN SUBSTITUTE ANY CRUMBLED CHEESE YOU LIKE FOR THE GOAT CHEESE. SOMETIMES I PREFER A NICE FETA, COTIJA, OR EVEN FROMAGE BLANC.

# CRUNCHY-ASS KALE CAESAR

Serves **4** • Prep Time: **5 minutes** • Cook Time: **5 minutes** • Total Time: **10 minutes**

**Craving some crunch? I got just what you need: a hearty, bold kale salad. Kale brings an earthy twist to this classic, and a homemade Greek yogurt-based dressing packs a protein punch to keep you fueled all day long. This salad means business. Plus, it's healthy as fuck. Kale is high in vitamins C, A, B6, and K (not to mention folate, fiber, and manganese). So go ahead and grab your tongs and get ready to toss together a salad that's anything but ordinary. It's time to believe in the power of greens.**

## INGREDIENTS

½ cup plain Greek yogurt
½ cup grated Parmesan
2 tablespoons extra-virgin olive oil
1 tablespoon Dijon mustard
1 teaspoon lemon zest
Juice of 1 lemon
1 teaspoon Worcestershire sauce
2 anchovy fillets
2 garlic cloves
6 cups kale, tough stems discarded and leaves roughly chopped
Salt and freshly ground pepper, to taste
Shaved parmesan, for topping

### SPECIAL EQUIPMENT

Food processor or blender

## METHOD

1 Make the dressing: Add the yogurt, Parmesan, olive oil, mustard, lemon zest, lemon juice, Worcestershire sauce, anchovies, and garlic to a food processor or blender. Process that shit until smooth.

2 In a big ass serving bowl, toss together the dressing and kale. Season with salt and pepper, sprinkle with shaved Parmesan, and enjoy!

# BALSAMICKY-ASS ARUGULA SALAD

Serves **4** • Prep Time: **8 minutes** • Cook Time: **None** • Total Time: **8 minutes**

**This dish is about to revolutionize your healthy eating routine. A mix of peppery arugula, juicy tomatoes, sharp onions, and crunchy sunflower seeds will make you forget you're eating a salad. With a tangy balsamic vinaigrette and sweet cara cara oranges, this salad hits all the spots for big flavor; And you know I know something about hitting spots.**

## INGREDIENTS

¼ cup cup extra-virgin olive oil
2 tablespoons fresh lemon juice
¼ cup red wine vinegar
1½ tablespoons Dijon mustard
1 tablespoon honey
2 medium garlic cloves, minced
½ teaspoon salt
Freshly ground black pepper, to taste
4 cups arugula
2 cups sliced red cabbage
10 cherry tomatoes, halved
¾ cup thinly sliced red onion
¼ cup roasted sunflower seeds
2 tablespoons aged balsamic vinegar, for drizzling
1 small cara cara orange, peeled and broken into segments

## METHOD

1. Make the dressing: add the oil, lemon juice, red wine vinegar, mustard, honey, garlic, and salt to a bowl and whisk until smooth, or blend in a blender if you're really about that life. Add pepper to taste.
2. In a big-ass bowl, toss together the arugula, cabbage, tomatoes, red onion, and sunflower seeds. Add the dressing and toss that shit with two large spoons.
3. Drizzle with the aged balsamic vinegar, drop in the orange slices, and serve it up.

## CHEETAH'S SECRET

**TO KICK IT UP A NOTCH, TRY MAKING MY ORANGE-BALSAMIC DRIZZLE:**

1 cup balsamic vinegar
¼ cup honey
Zest of 1 orange
1 sprig fresh thyme (optional)
Pinch of salt

1. In a small saucepan, combine the balsamic vinegar, honey, orange zest, thyme (if using), and a pinch of salt.
2. Bring the mixture to a boil over medium-high heat, stirring occasionally.
3. Reduce the heat to medium-low and let the mixture simmer gently until reduced by half, about 15 to 20 minutes. The mixture should be syrupy and thick enough to coat the back of a spoon.
4. Remove the saucepan from heat and let the orange balsamic drizzle cool to room temperature.
5. Transfer the drizzle to an airtight container and store in the refrigerator for up to 2 weeks.

# CRUCIFEROUS-ASS BRUSSELS SPROUT SALAD

Serves 4 • Prep Time: 5 minutes • Cook Time: 25 minutes • Total Time: 30 minutes

**Say hello to this badass Brussels sprout salad, a dish that's about to make you fall in love with these little green, nutritious balls of goodness. We're talking roasted Brussels sprouts mingling with thinly sliced red onions and crunchy hazelnuts, tossed in a tangy vinaigrette and finished with a rich balsamic reduction. Ideal for any occasion where you want to impress with minimal effort, this salad will turn heads and convert even the biggest Brussels sprout skeptics into Brussels sprout devotees.**

## INGREDIENTS

- 1 pound (454g) Brussels sprouts, halved and tough outer leaves removed
- ¼ cup extra-virgin olive oil for dressing, plus 1 tablespoon for cooking
- 1 teaspoon salt, plus more to taste
- 1 teaspoon freshly ground pepper, plus more to taste
- ¼ cup white balsamic vinegar
- 1 tablespoon honey
- 1 teaspoon fresh orange zest
- 2 teaspoons Dijon mustard
- ½ cup hazelnuts
- 3 tablespoons dried cranberries
- ¼ medium red onion, thinly sliced
- 1 tablespoon balsamic glaze

## METHOD

1. Preheat the oven to 425°F (220°C) and line a baking sheet with foil.
2. Arrange the sprouts in a single layer on the prepared baking sheet and toss with 1 tablespoon olive oil. Sprinkle that shit with salt and pepper. Bake for 20 minutes or until golden. Remove and reduce the oven temperature to 350°F (175°C).
3. Meanwhile, make the glaze: Bring the balsamic vinegar and honey to a light boil in a small saucepan over medium-high heat. Reduce to low and simmer for 13 to 16 minutes or until thick enough to coat the back of a spoon. Stir in the orange zest. Set aside.
4. Next, make the vinaigrette: In a small bowl, whisk together the balsamic reduction, ¼ cup olive oil, and the Dijon mustard. Season with salt and pepper to taste.
5. Add the hazelnuts to a clean baking sheet and bake for 3 to 4 minutes or until fragrant. Set aside to cool for 2 to 3 minutes, then roughly chop.
6. Toss the sprouts, dried cranberries, and onion together in a big-ass bowl with the vinaigrette. Sprinkle hazelnuts over top and drizzle with extra balsamic glaze and prepare for a cruciferous flavor bomb!

## CHEETAH'S SECRET

FOR SOME EXTRA PIZZAZZ, TOP WITH GARLIC CONFIT. HERE'S MY SIMPLE RECIPE:

- 1 cup garlic cloves, peeled
- 1 cup olive oil
- Fresh thyme, rosemary, or peppercorns (optional)

1. Preheat the oven to 200°F (95°C).
2. Place the garlic in a small, oven-safe dish and cover with oil (you may need more than 1 cup, depending on your dish). Add in any optional herbs or seasonings. Cover with aluminum foil and cook, undisturbed, for 1½ to 2 hours, or until the garlic cloves are tender and golden brown.
3. Allow to cool to room temperature before using. Store in an airtight container for up to two weeks in the fridge.

# YUMMY-ASS CABBAGE AND PEANUT SLAW

Serves 4 • Prep Time: 10 minutes • Cook Time: None • Total Time: 10 minutes (plus chilling time)

**This Yummy-Ass Cabbage And Peanut Slaw is a tangy, nutty, umami bomb that's perfect for picnics, backyard barbecues, and potlucks. It is as easy to make as it is to devour. The cabbage brings the crunch, the peanuts add a delightful nutty twist, and the dressing ties it all together. Noah once brought this to his family reunion, and it was so good, they let him stay. So skip the boring coleslaw and get ready to whip up this ultimate crowd-pleaser.**

## INGREDIENTS

1 cup unsalted peanuts
½ teaspoon salt
3 tablespoons rice vinegar
2 tablespoons sesame oil
1 tablespoon granulated sugar
1 tablespoon soy sauce
1 tablespoon creamy peanut butter (optional)
1 medium cabbage, cored and finely shredded
1½ cups chopped scallions
1¼ cups chopped fresh cilantro
Salt and freshly ground pepper, to taste
1 tablespoon sesame seeds

## METHOD

1. In a large, dry skillet over medium heat, toast the peanuts with ½ teaspoon of salt until lightly golden and fragrant, for 2 to 3 minutes, stirring every 15 seconds. Remove from heat and let those nuts cool.
2. In a small bowl, whisk together the rice vinegar, sesame oil, sugar, soy sauce, and peanut butter (if using) until the sugar has dissolved.
3. Add the cabbage, toasted peanuts, scallions, and cilantro to a serving bowl.
4. Pour the vinegar-oil mixture over the cabbage mixture and toss until everything is well coated. Season with salt and pepper to taste.
5. Cover and refrigerate for 30 minutes or up to 2 hours to allow those flavors to mingle a little before digging in.
6. Before serving, sprinkle with sesame seeds.

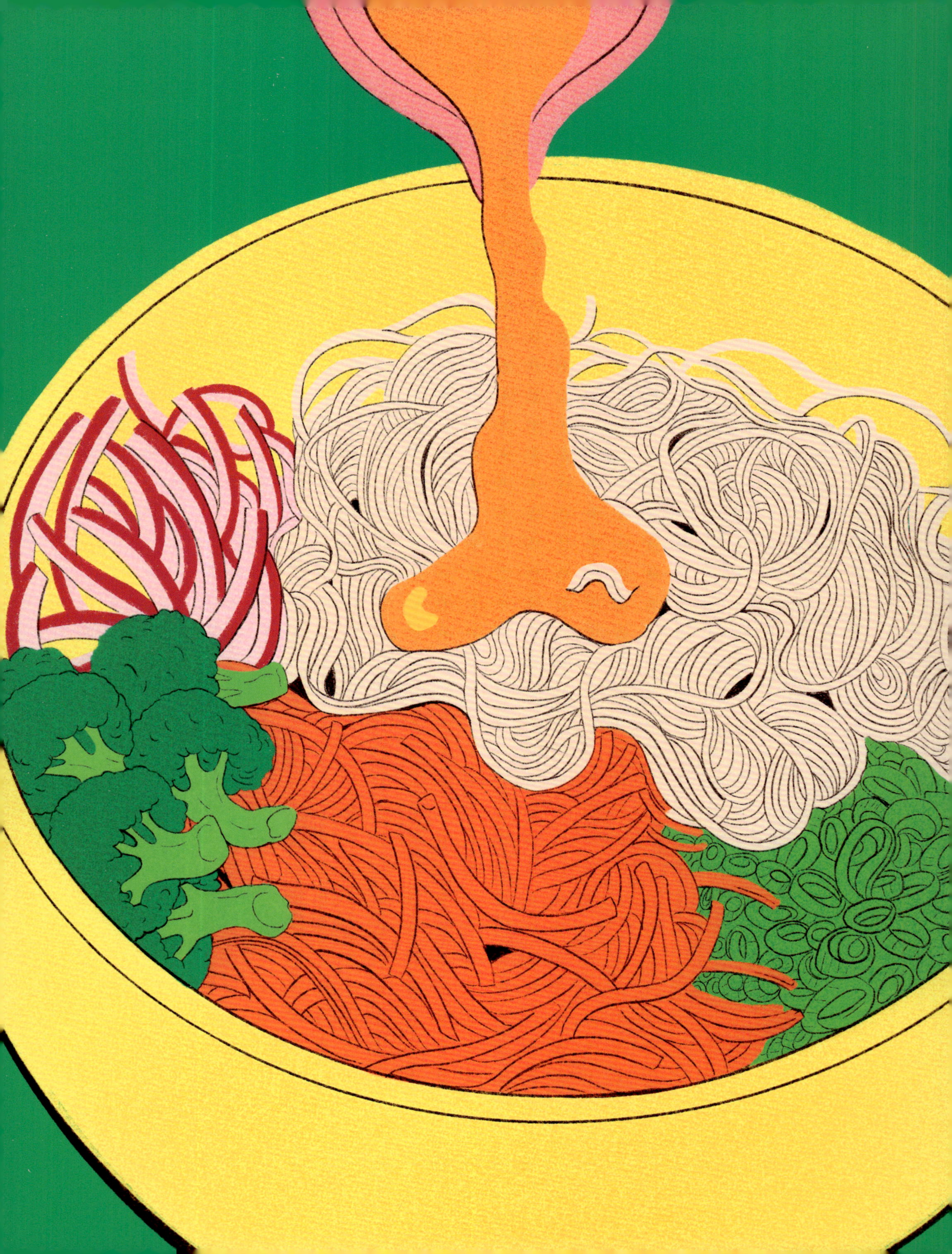

# NOODLEY-ASS SOBA NOODLE SALAD

Serves 2 • Prep Time: 6 minutes • Cook Time: See package directions • Total Time: 6 minutes

This recipe combines tender soba noodles with crisp carrots, crunchy broccoli, and a tangy Asian-inspired dressing that'll make your taste buds sing. This is one of my all-time favorites for a summer night, since it can be served chilled. Speaking of chilled, pair it with your favorite sake or white wine. Then, sit back, relax, and let those fresh flavors bust a move on your tongue.

## INGREDIENTS

1× 8-ounce (227g) package soba noodles
1 cup chopped broccoli
1 cup matchstick carrots
¼ medium red onion, thinly sliced
¼ cup diced cucumber
1 birds eye chili, seeded and chopped
½ cup chopped fresh cilantro
1 teaspoon sesame oil
1 tablespoon dark soy sauce
Juice of 1 small lime
1 scallion, sliced
¼ cup chopped peanuts
Sesame seeds, for garnish

## METHOD

1. Bring a large pot of water to a boil. Cook the soba noodles according to the package instructions. Drain and rinse under cold water to stop the cooking process. Set aside.
2. Meanwhile, steam the broccoli for 2 to 3 minutes until slightly tender but still crisp. Rinse under cold water to stop the cooking process and drain well.
3. In a large mixing bowl, combine the cooked soba noodles, steamed broccoli, carrots, red onion, cucumber, bird's eye chili, and cilantro.
4. In a small bowl, whisk together the sesame oil, dark soy sauce, and lime juice until well combined.
5. Pour the soy sauce mixture over the soba-vegetable mixture. Toss until evenly coated.
6. Top the salad with sliced scallions, chopped peanuts, and sesame seeds.
7. For best flavor, cover the salad and refrigerate for at least 30 minutes to allow the flavors to meld together before serving.
8. Serve chilled or at room temperature and enjoy!

# PEACHY-ASS TOMATO AND BURRATA SALAD

Serves 4 • Prep Time: 5 minutes • Cook Time: None • Total Time: 5 minutes

This one time on a farm outside of Columbus, Georgia, I was served a version of this dish after a weekend of epic fornication with Mary Lynn, a southern belle with the juiciest peach you've ever seen. I don't know what I enjoyed more—this salad or Mary Lynn. Prepare your palate to be dazzled by summer's finest. This recipe brings together juicy peaches, vibrant heirloom tomatoes, and creamy burrata, with fresh basil and mint. It's all balanced with a splash of balsamic glaze. It's a symphony of sweet, savory, and tangy flavors. Enjoy every luscious, juicy bite and watch as this dish becomes the star of your summer table.

## INGREDIENTS

- 3 large ripe peaches, peeled, pitted, and sliced
- 1 large heirloom tomato, sliced
- 1 pint cherry tomatoes, halved
- 8 ounces (226g) fresh burrata
- ½ cup thinly sliced basil leaves
- ¼ cup thinly sliced mint leaves
- ¼ cup extra-virgin olive oil
- 3 tablespoons balsamic glaze
- Flaky salt and freshly ground black pepper, to taste

## METHOD

1. Arrange the heirloom tomato and peach slices on a big ass serving platter, alternating between peach and tomato. Then scatter the halved cherry tomatoes across the platter—as Nancy Silverton says, it should look like it fell from the sky.
2. Place the burrata in the center, so the other ingredients surround it like a delicious, summery halo.
3. Sprinkle the basil and mint over the top of the whole platter. Drizzle with olive oil and balsamic glaze, and finish with flaky salt and pepper.

## CHEETAH'S SECRET

WANT TO MAKE THIS EXTRA FANCY? DRIZZLE ON LOCAL HONEY, ADD TOASTED PINE NUTS, AND SERVE WITH TOASTED BAGUETTE SLICES.

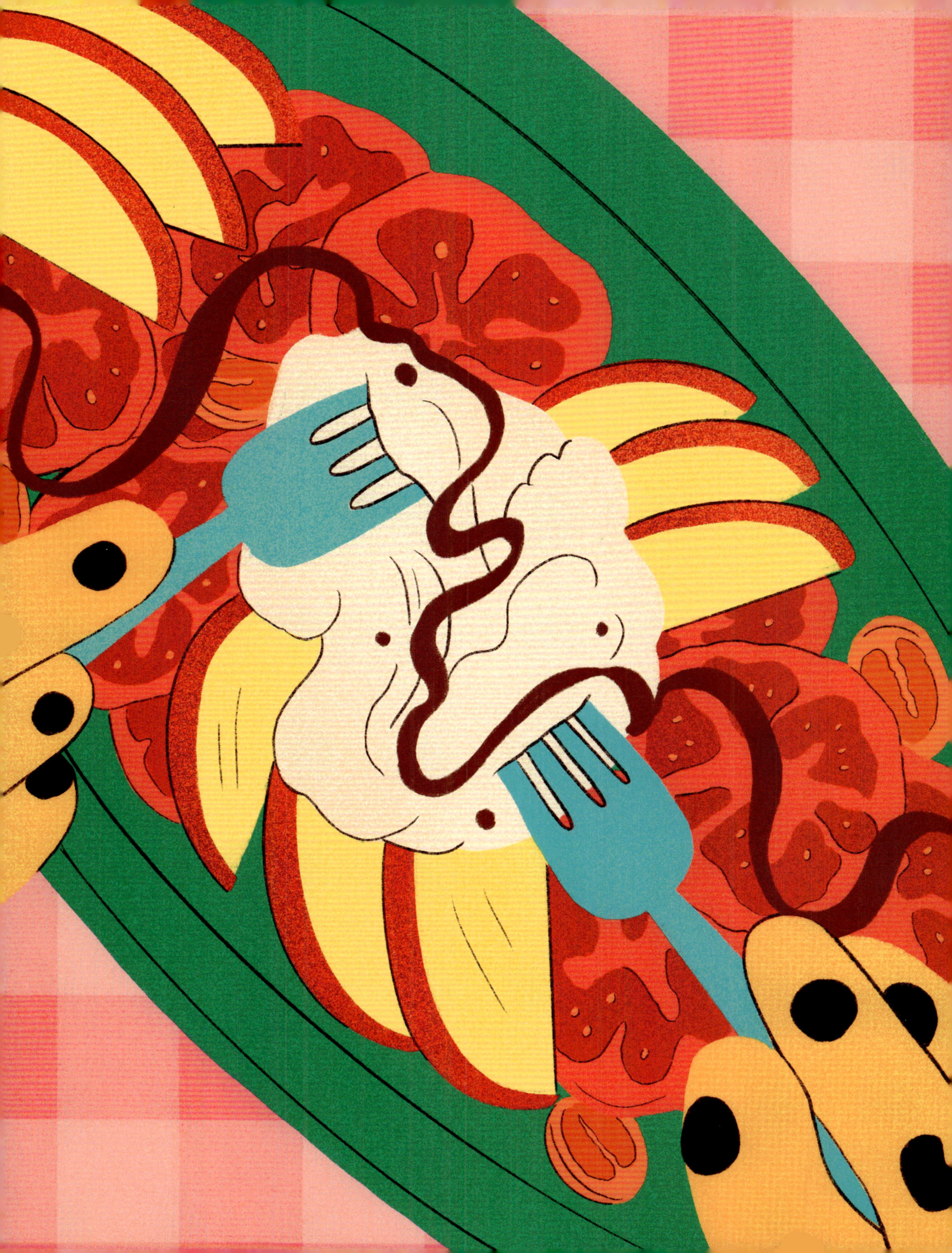

# CRISPY-ASS FARRO, ARUGULA, AND APPLE SALAD

Serves 4 to 5 • Prep Time: 5 minutes • Cook Time: 30 minutes • Total Time: 35 minutes

This is a fall favorite in my neck of the jungle. The crisp apple juxtaposes the chewy farro, with peppery arugula and zesty lemon vinaigrette slapping you in the mouth with a burst of bright flavors. The tanginess of the Pecorino Romano takes this salad to a whole new level. If there was a salad hall of fame, this would definitely be in it.

## INGREDIENTS

1 cup semi-pearled farro
1× 5-ounce (142g) package arugula
1 Honeycrisp apple, cored and thinly sliced
2 chopped scallions
3 tablespoons fresh lemon juice
4 tablespoons extra-virgin olive oil
3 tablespoons finely chopped fresh mint
½ cup shaved Pecorino Romano
Flaky sea salt, to taste
Freshly ground black pepper, to taste

## METHOD

1. Prepare the farro according to package directions (it should take 20 to 30 minutes). Drain and allow to cool to room temperature so it won't wilt the arugula.
2. In a large-ass serving bowl, toss together the arugula, farro, apple, scallions, 2 tablespoons of the lemon juice, and 2 tablespoons of the olive oil.
3. Drizzle the remaining olive oil and lemon juice over the top. Sprinkle with the mint, Pecorino Romano, salt, and pepper. Enjoy!

## CHEETAH'S SECRET

THIS SALAD CAN CHANGE WITH THE SEASONS. DURING SUMMER, CONSIDER ADDING BLACKBERRIES INSTEAD OF APPLES. IN WINTER, TRY POMEGRANATE OR BLOOD ORANGES. AND IN SPRING, TRY STRAWBERRIES.

# BURNT-ASS BROCCOLI RABE

## with Halloumi, Watercress, and Blackberry Vinaigrette

Serves **4** • Prep Time: **8 minutes** • Cook Time: **17 minutes** • Total Time: **25 minutes**

**This vibrant mix of tender broccoli rabe, peppery watercress, and grilled halloumi cheese, all dressed up with a tangy, sweet blackberry vinaigrette is a combination that is both unique and delicious. The bittersweet broccoli rabe pairs perfectly with the salty, squeaky halloumi, while the fresh watercress adds a crisp bite. Drizzle it all with the blackberry vinaigrette, and you've got a dish that's bold and beautiful, like Noah's favorite TV show. It's the ultimate proof that salads can be adventurous and packed with personality. Enjoy every flavorful, tangy, and savory bite as you elevate your salad repertoire and impress anyone who tries it.**

### INGREDIENTS

#### FOR THE SALAD

1 tablespoon avocado oil
1 bunch broccoli rabe, ends and leaves trimmed
1 large garlic clove, minced
½ teaspoon crushed red pepper flakes
Pinch of salt
1 tablespoon fresh lemon juice
7 ounces halloumi cheese, cut into ½-inch (1cm) slices
1 cup watercress, washed and dried

#### FOR THE DRESSING

½ cup fresh blackberries
½ teaspoon freshly ground pepper, plus more to taste
½ cup extra-virgin olive oil
⅓ cup red wine vinegar
1 tablespoon fresh lemon juice
½ tablespoon Dijon mustard
Flaky sea salt, to taste

#### SPECIAL EQUIPMENT

Grill or grill pan
Food processor or blender

### METHOD

1 Preheat the oven to 350°F (175°C).

2 Add the avocado oil to a large skillet over medium-high heat. Once shimmering, add the broccoli rabe, garlic, crushed red pepper, salt, and lemon juice. Cook, stirring occasionally, until the broccoli rabe is tender and charred in spots, about 5 to 7 minutes. Set aside to cool.

3 Get your grill nice and hot—about 400°F (200°C) (You can also use a grill pan). Lightly spray or brush the halloumi slices with olive oil then grill them until golden grill marks appear, about 2 minutes on each side.

4 Line a baking sheet with parchment paper.

5 Make the dressing: in a large-ass bowl, gently mix the blackberries and black pepper. Transfer the mixture to the prepared baking sheet and spread into a single layer. Cook for 5 to 7 minutes or until soft and juicy. Remove from the oven and let cool slightly, about 2 minutes.

6 Add the berries and juice from the tray to a food processor or blender. Pour in the vinegar, mustard, and olive oil and process that shit until smooth. Taste and adjust pepper and vinegar levels to your liking.

7 Arrange the watercress on the bottom, layer the broccoli rabe on top for a visually stunning presentation, then top with halloumi and drizzle with vinaigrette. Top it off with a pinch of flaky sea salt and enjoy.

# ALL THE PASTA-BILITIES

# AUTHENTIC-ASS TAGLIATELLE

## from Scratch

Serves **4** • Prep Time: **15 minutes (plus 30 minutes resting time)** • Cook Time: **None** • Total Time: **45 minutes**

**Welcome to the art of making handcrafted pasta—a culinary experience that connects you to the rich tradition of Italian cuisine. There's something deeply satisfying about transforming simple ingredients like flour and eggs into silky ribbons of pasta. Whether you're a seasoned cook or a kitchen novice, making tagliatelle from scratch is a delightful journey from dough to dish. Feel free to use this dough for any pasta shape you'd like to make—there are hundreds!**

### INGREDIENTS

2 cups all-purpose flour
3 large eggs
Pinch of salt

### METHOD

TRY THIS!

1. Place the flour in a pile on a clean surface. Use your fingers to make a well in the center. Crack the eggs into the well, and use a fork to lightly beat the eggs. Then, slowly bring in flour from around the outside and combine with the eggs, but be careful to maintain the flour walls so your egg doesn't spill out. Once the eggs are no longer runny and a dough starts to form, incorporate the sides of the well and gently press everything into a nice ball.
2. Knead the dough until completely smooth, about 7 to 10 minutes. If your dough is sticky, add a light dusting of flour and knead until incorporated.
3. Wrap in plastic wrap and allow to rest at room temperature for 30 minutes.
4. Divide dough into 4 equal portions. Place one portion of dough on a lightly floured surface. Re-cover the remaining dough. Roll the uncovered dough into a paper-thin rectangle. Fold dough once like an envelope and cut vertically into ½-inch to 1-inch (1.27 cm to 2.54 cm) strips. Repeat with remaining dough portions.
5. Once your pasta is all cut, dust them with some extra flour and let them chill for 15 to 20 minutes to dry out a little bit.
6. To cook, bring a large pot of water to a boil, add a pinch of salt, and cook pasta for 2 to 3 minutes. Drain and enjoy with your favorite sauce or toppings.

# SUNFLOWER PESTO-ASS PAPPARDELLE

Serves 4 • Prep Time: 5 minutes • Cook Time: 12 minutes • Total Time: 17 minutes

This vibrant twist on classic pesto pasta promises to save on funds without compromising on flavor. Forget pine nuts; you don't need to spend a million dollars on some little-ass nuts. Just grab some sunflower seeds and you're on your way to pesto paradise. This recipe is perfect for a quick weeknight dinner or a fancy feast. The sunflower pesto is herbaceous, aromatic, tangy, and packed with flavor, blending beautifully with al dente pasta for a meal that's comforting and refreshing.

## INGREDIENTS

⅓ cup raw, shelled sunflower seeds

2 cups loosely packed fresh basil leaves

3 garlic cloves

4 ounces (113g) Parmesan, cut into chunks

½ cup olive oil

Juice from 1 lemon

1 teaspoon salt

½ teaspoon freshly ground pepper

16 ounces (450g) pappardelle pasta

## METHOD

1. In a small, dry pan over medium heat, toast the sunflower seeds, stirring constantly, until aromatic and golden brown, about 4 minutes. Remove from the heat and let that shit cool.
2. Place the basil, sunflower seeds, garlic, Parmesan chunks, olive oil, lemon juice, salt, and pepper in a food processor and process until you reach your desired smoothness (I like it mostly smooth with a few small chunks here and there for texture. But trust your gut!).
3. Cook the pasta according to the package directions. Reserve a ½ cup of the pasta water and then drain the rest.
4. Return the pasta to the pot it was cooked in. Set the heat to low and add in the pesto and toss to coat. Mix in some of the reserved pasta water and cook, stirring often, until the pesto is warm, about 3 minutes.
5. Serve and enjoy.

### CHEETAH'S SECRET

DON'T HAVE SUNFLOWER SEEDS? YOU CAN USE WHATEVER NUTS YOU HAVE IN THE HOUSE. SUB OUT THE SEEDS FOR ALMONDS, WALNUTS, OR EVEN PISTACHIOS IF THAT'S HOW YOU ROLL!

# STUFFED-ASS MUSHROOM RICOTTA RAVIOLI

## with White Wine Sauce

Serves 6 to 8 • Prep Time: 95 minutes • Cook Time: 25 minutes • Total Time: 2 hours

These ravioli are so stuffed, they'll make your Thanksgiving turkey jealous. Packed to the brim with a luscious blend of mushrooms and ricotta, these ravioli are the pasta equivalent of a mic drop. The simple yet decadent white wine sauce is so smooth and delicious, that if you serve these for date night you'll get jealous of the pleasure it gives to your significant other. Now enough with the chatter, let's get stuffing.

### INGREDIENTS

7 tablespoons unsalted butter, divided

8 ounces (226g) baby bella mushrooms, diced

1 tablespoon finely chopped fresh thyme

1 teaspoon finely chopped fresh sage

15 ounces (425g) ricotta cheese

1 teaspoon salt

1 teaspoon freshly ground pepper

1× batch Authentic-Ass Tagliatelle dough (see page 106)

1 tablespoon chopped chives

¼ cup olive oil

2 teaspoons minced garlic

1½ teaspoons salt

½ teaspoon crushed red pepper flakes (optional)

½ cup white wine

Chopped chives, for serving

#### SPECIAL EQUIPMENT

Rolling pin

Pasta cutter or pastry wheel

### METHOD

1. Make the filling: Heat a big-ass frying pan over medium heat. Add 2 tablespoons of the butter or olive oil. Once melted/shimmering, add the mushrooms, thyme, sage, and cook, stirring frequently, for 3 minutes. Remove from the pan and let it cool slightly in a large bowl.
2. Add the ricotta, salt, and pepper to the bowl with the mushrooms. Stir to combine.
3. Prepare the pasta: Follow the tagliatelle recipe (page 106) through step 3. Place the dough on a lightly floured surface. Use a rolling pin to roll out the dough into one large ⅛-inch (3mm) thick rectangle. Cut the sheet in half, then spoon a ½ teaspoon of filling at 1-inch (2.5cm) intervals along the center of the rectangle (if you're looking at the rectangle lengthwise), starting (and finishing) 1 inch (2.5cm) from the edge. Moisten the edges of the sheet with water and place the other pasta sheet on top. Use your fingers to press along each mound of filling, gently sealing the ravioli and pushing out any air. With a pasta cutter or pastry wheel, cut into 1½ inch (4cm) squares. If using a pastry wheel, you will need to crimp the edges of your ravioli with the back of a fork. Let sit uncovered to dry while you prepare the sauce.
4. In a large saucepan, heat the olive oil over medium heat. Add the red pepper (if using) and garlic and cook until the garlic is fragrant, about 30 seconds. Add the butter, wine, and salt. Cook, stirring constantly, for 1½ to 2 minutes. Remove from the heat.
5. Meanwhile, bring a large pot of water to boil over high heat. Add the ravioli and cook for 2 to 3 minutes or until it floats.
6. Drain pasta, add to sauce and toss to coat. Plate with a sprinkle of chives and fresh black pepper.

## CHEETAH'S SECRET

YOU CAN USE ANY SAUCE YOU LIKE FOR THIS RAVIOLI. TRY IT IN A SAGE BUTTER SAUCE OR A SIMPLE TOMATO SAUCE, OR YOU CAN MAKE IT EVEN EASIER WITH A SIMPLE OLIVE OIL AND GARLIC SAUCE. SIMPLY HEAT SOME OLIVE OIL IN A SKILLET OVER MEDIUM HEAT WITH SOME SLICED GARLIC AND CRUSHED RED PEPPER! THE BEST WAY TO PREPARE THE RAVIOLI IS AS ABOVE, BOIL UNTIL THE PASTA IS ALMOST AL DENTE, THEN LET IT FINISH COOKING IN A HOT SKILLET WITH YOUR SAUCE OF CHOICE.

# RICH-ASS BACON AND SUN-DRIED TOMATO PASTA

Serves **8** • Prep Time: **5 minutes** • Cook Time: **5 minutes** • Total Time: **10 minutes**

**This dish is the ultimate comfort food, combining crispy bacon, sweet and tangy sun-dried tomatoes, and a decadent cream sauce that clings to every strand of pasta like a long, passionate kiss. It's the kind of meal that makes you forget your troubles and embrace the bliss of indulgence. Perfect for a cozy night in or when you want to impress without the stress, this pasta is guaranteed to become a favorite in your culinary repertoire!**

## INGREDIENTS

16 ounces (454g) rigatoni
8 ounces bacon, chopped
1× 3 ounce (85g) package sun-dried tomatoes, julienne cut
4 tablespoons heavy cream
3 tablespoons Parmigiano Reggiano, divided
3 tablespoons fresh basil, roughly torn
½ teaspoon freshly ground pepper

## METHOD

1. Cook pasta according to box directions. Drain and save about a ½ cup of the pasta water.
2. Add the chopped bacon to a sauté pan set over medium heat and cook, stirring often, until golden brown, about 6 minutes. Drain all but about 1 tablespoon of the grease and return the pan to the stove (the bacon should still be in the pan).
3. Add the tomatoes and cook for 2 minutes, stirring every 30 seconds.
4. Add in the heavy cream and 2 tablespoons of the Parmigiano Reggiano. Stir to combine. Add the pasta and the reserved pasta water, 2 tablespoons at a time. Cook until the rigatoni is beautifully coated and the sauce sticks to it.
5. Serve in bowls and top with basil, the remaining cheese, and black pepper.

## CHEETAH'S SECRET

IF YOU'RE CRAVING SOME PROTEIN, I LOVE TOPPING THIS PASTA WITH GRILLED, SLICED CHICKEN. THE TENDER CHICKEN AND CREAMY SAUCE ARE A MATCH MADE IN HEAVEN.

# CHEESY-ASS 4 CHEESE MAC 'N' CHEESE

Serves **12** • Prep Time: **5 minutes** • Cook Time: **37 minutes** • Total Time: **42 minutes**

I discovered this recipe when I spent a summer in the sweltering South Carolina heat. I was at a barbeque with all the succulent, smoked, charred, and grilled meat in the world, but this mac 'n' cheese was the talk of the party, and for a good reason—it's to die for. The four cheeses blend together to create the creamiest bite of Americana you'll ever have. Bring it to Thanksgiving to impress your in-laws, or simply make it for a comforting weeknight dinner. Either way, you're in for a hell of a treat, and a LOT of compliments.

## INGREDIENTS

1 pound uncooked elbow macaroni

1 cup half and half

1 cup heavy whipping cream

4 tablespoons unsalted butter

1¼ cups shredded sharp cheddar

1¼ cups shredded mozzarella

1¼ cups shredded mild cheddar

1¼ cup Velveeta (cut into chunks), plus more for sprinkling

2 tablespoons granulated sugar

½ teaspoon garlic salt

½ teaspoon seasoned salt (such as Lawry's)

1 tablespoon yellow mustard

### SPECIAL EQUIPMENT

9×13-inch (23×33 cm) baking dish

## METHOD

1. First thing's first, preheat the oven to 375°F (190°C).
2. Cook macaroni according to package directions and set aside (see Note).
3. Add the half and half, heavy cream, butter, cheeses, sugar, garlic salt, seasoned salt, and mustard to a large pot. Bring to a simmer over medium heat, stirring frequently. Cook until all the cheese has melted and the mixture is smooth as hell.
4. Add the noodles to a large, heatproof bowl. Pour the cheese mixture over the noodles and gently stir to coat. Taste and adjust seasonings as needed.
5. Pour the noodles into the baking dish, add the remaining Velveeta (you can also sprinkle more of the cheddar on top if you want), and give it one more mix. Cover with foil and bake for 12 to 15 minutes. Uncover and cook for an additional 7 minutes.
6. Allow to cool slightly and enjoy.

***Note:** Don't forget to salt the water!*

## CHEETAH'S SECRET

TO GIVE YOUR MAC 'N' CHEESE AN EXTRA BIT OF TEXTURE, TOP WITH PANKO BREAD CRUMBS BEFORE BAKING.

# PUMPKINY-ASS GNOCCHI

## with Garlicky Brown Butter Sage Sauce

Serves 4 • Prep Time: 30 minutes • Cook Time: 10 minutes • Total Time: 40 minutes

**Looking for the ultimate fall pasta dish? Well, here it is: Soft, pillowy clouds of pasta made with sweet, earthy carrots bring a vibrant twist to a classic favorite. Tossed in a rich, golden butter sauce with a hint of fresh herbs, this meal will have you yelling, "Cheetah, I need seconds!"**

### INGREDIENTS

#### FOR THE GNOCCHI

1 cup pumpkin purée (canned or homemade, make sure you drain well if watery)

¾ cup ricotta, well-drained

1 large egg, lightly beaten

½ cup grated Parmesan, plus 2 tablespoons for serving

1 teaspoon salt

¼ teaspoon freshly grated nutmeg

1½ to 2 cups all-purpose flour, plus extra for dusting

#### FOR THE SAUCE

4 tablespoons unsalted butter

2 to 3 garlic cloves, thinly sliced (⅛ inch [3mm] thick, at most)

6 fresh sage leaves

Salt and freshly ground pepper, to taste

### METHOD

1. Make the gnocchi: in a large ass mixing bowl, combine the pumpkin purée, ricotta, egg, Parmesan, salt, and nutmeg. Mix until as smooth as one of my famous pick-up lines.
2. Add the flour, ½ cup at a time, mixing gently until a soft dough forms. The dough should be slightly sticky but manageable. Avoid overworking it or the dough will turn out dense.
3. Turn the dough out onto a floured surface. Divide it into 4 portions. Roll each portion into a rope about ¾-inch thick, then cut into 1-inch (2.5cm) pieces (If you wanna get all fancy, you can roll each piece over the back of a fork or gnocchi board to create ridges.) Dust lightly with flour to prevent sticking.
4. Bring a large pot of salted water to a gentle boil. Drop the gnocchi in batches, stirring to prevent any sticking. When the gnocchi float to the surface (about 2 to 3 minutes), let them cook for 30 seconds more, then remove with a slotted spoon. Transfer to a plate or tray and keep warm.
5. Prepare the sauce: in a large skillet over medium heat, melt the butter. Swirl the pan occasionally as the butter begins to bubble and turn golden brown, releasing a nutty aroma.
6. Add the sliced garlic to the browned butter and cook for about 1 minute, stirring frequently, until the garlic is fragrant and lightly golden.
7. Add the sage leaves and cook for 30 seconds to 1 minute, until crispy.
8. Add the cooked gnocchi to the skillet, tossing gently to coat them in the garlicky brown butter sage sauce. Cook for 1 minute to let the flavors meld.
9. Divide the gnocchi among the plates, drizzle with remaining sauce from the pan, and sprinkle with grated Parmesan.
10. Serve immediately, and watch it disappear.

# CREAMY-ASS SCALLION CREAM BUCATINI

Serves 5 to 6 • Prep Time: 5 minutes • Cook Time: 12 minutes • Total Time: 17 minutes

This is a pasta with personality. Its' luscious, velvety sauce wraps around every strand of bucatini like a clingy girlfriend, but it's the opposite of annoying. With the fresh, vibrant kick of scallions adding a punch of flavor, this pasta is anything but ordinary. It's rich, it's indulgent, and it's got attitude—perfect for when you want a meal that's comforting but with a little edge.

## INGREDIENTS

1 cup heavy cream
½ cup frozen peas, thawed
1 cup scallions, chopped, divided
Freshly ground pepper
16 ounces (454g) bucatini
Pinch of salt
1 cup grated Pecorino Romano
2 tablespoons fresh lemon juice

### SPECIAL EQUIPMENT

Blender

## METHOD

1. In a large, deep pan over medium-low heat, add the heavy cream, peas, ¾ cup chopped scallions, and freshly ground pepper. Cook for 5 to 7 minutes or until peas are softened.
2. Transfer to a blender and blend on low until silky smooth, about 3 minutes. Return the sauce to the pan.
3. Prepare noodles according to package directions (and don't forget to salt your water no matter what that box says!), but make sure to remove pasta 2 minutes BEFORE it becomes al dente. Drain (save some pasta water!) and add to the skillet with the cream sauce and 4 tbsp of that pasta water. Stir in the Pecorino Romano. If the sauce is too thick, add up to ½ cup of pasta water, 1 tablespoon at a time, to thin it out. The pasta should absorb the green color of the sauce.
4. Remove from heat, and serve with freshly ground pepper, garnishing with the remaining scallions.

## CHEETAH'S SECRET

THIS IS A GREAT WAY TO USE UP ANY HERBS YOU HAVE LYING AROUND LIKE MINT, PARSLEY, OR CILANTRO. FEEL FREE TO USE PARMESAN INSTEAD OF PECORINO ROMANO IF THAT'S WHAT YOU HAVE—THIS IS MORE OF A GUIDELINE RECIPE THAN SOMETHING THAT IS SET IN STONE!

# SEXY-ASS SPAGHETTI ALL'ASSASSINA

Serves 4 • Prep Time: 2 minutes • Cook Time: 8 to 10 minutes • Total Time: 10 to 12 minutes

**Spaghetti all'Assassina isn't just a dish—it's an experience, a seductive plate of pasta that's got some serious heat. This isn't your grandma's spaghetti; it's bold, fiery, and ready to make your taste buds tingle with excitement. The dry pasta is cooked directly in a spicy tomato sauce until it's deliciously caramelized, so every bite packs a punch—hence the name "Assassin's Spaghetti." This dish is for those who like to live on the edge, flirting with danger while twirling their fork. So light some candles, pour a glass of wine, and get ready for a spicy pasta that oozes with sensuality.**

## INGREDIENTS

- 2 tablespoons olive oil, plus more for serving
- 2 garlic cloves, thinly sliced
- 2 tablespoons crushed red pepper flakes (optional)
- 16 ounces (454g) spaghetti
- 1× 15-ounce can crushed tomatoes
- 1 teaspoon salt
- 1 tablespoon chopped fresh flat-leaf parsley

## METHOD

1. Heat the olive oil, garlic slices, and pepper flakes in a big-ass pan over medium-high heat for 1 minute.
2. Spread out the uncooked, dry pasta in a single layer in the pan on top of the oil and pepper flakes.
3. Mix 2 cups of crushed tomatoes and 1 cup of hot water. Pour that shit over the pasta. It is imperative not to disturb the pasta—it's taking a nap, and you don't want to wake an assassin while it sleeps. Trust me. Let him cook.
4. Once most of the liquid is absorbed (about 8 to 10 minutes), use tongs to "flip" the pasta pieces over so that they can cook on the other side. Cook, undisturbed for 2 to 2½ minutes. The pasta should begin to pop and sizzle.
5. Now, add the remaining 1 cup of tomatoes. Reduce the heat to medium and cook, continuously stirring and flipping until the noodles are coated, the sauce is mostly absorbed, and the pasta is al dente, about 3 minutes. Stir in salt.
6. Serve with a drizzle of olive oil, chopped parsley and enjoy.

# LEMONY-ASS CAPER SPAGHETTI

## with Pan-Seared Chicken

Serves 3 to 4 • Prep Time: 5 minutes • Cook Time: 15 minutes • Total Time: 20 minutes

**Get ready for some serious flavor with this tender pasta drenched in a tangy, zesty lemon-caper sauce that's got just the right amount of attitude. Paired with juicy, perfectly pan-seared chicken, it's like a Mediterranean vacation in your mouth—no passport required. This recipe is so easy and delicious, it's sure to become a staple in your kitchen. I make this quite literally every week, and I never hear Noah complaining. So grab your apron, turn up the heat, and let's get this flavor party started!**

### INGREDIENTS

16 ounces (454g) spaghetti
2 medium boneless, skinless chicken breasts
1 teaspoon garlic powder
1 teaspoon onion powder
1 teaspoon salt
1 teaspoon freshly ground pepper
¼ cup, plus 1 tablespoon olive oil, divided
3 garlic cloves, thinly sliced
½ teaspoon crushed red pepper flakes
½ cup Parmesan, divided
3 tablespoons capers
1 teaspoon lemon zest
Juice of 1 lemon
2 tablespoons roughly chopped fresh flat-leaf parsley, for garnish

### METHOD

1. Cook the spaghetti according to the package directions. Turn off the heat, reserve ¼ cup of the cooking water, then drain the pasta, and set it aside
2. Meanwhile, pat the chicken breasts completely dry.
3. Mix the garlic powder, onion powder, salt, and pepper in a small-ass bowl.
4. Rub that chicken down with 1 tablespoon of the olive oil. Then, sprinkle it all over with the seasoning mix.
5. Heat a big-ass pan over medium-high heat. Add 1 tablespoon of olive oil. Once shimmering, add the chicken to the pan and cook, undisturbed, for 5 minutes. Flip and continue cooking until cooked through, about 4 to 7 minutes. Transfer to a plate.
6. In the same pan over medium-low heat, add ¼ cup olive oil along with the garlic, capers, and red pepper flakes. Cook for 1 minute until fragrant, then add the lemon zest. Cook for 30 seconds then pour in the lemon juice slowly, stirring vigorously for 2 minutes.
7. Add the pasta and half of the Parmesan to the sauce and stir until the pasta is evenly coated. If the sauce is too thick, add some pasta water to thin it out.
8. Slice the chicken into strips and add it to the pasta. Add the capers, lemon zest, and lemon juice, and give it a toss. Serve and enjoy!

### CHEETAH'S SECRET

THIS RECIPE ALSO WORKS WELL WITH BONELESS, SKINLESS CHICKEN THIGHS OR PORK TENDERLOIN. TRY SERVING WITH SOME CHOPPED AND PAN-FRIED PROSCIUTTO ON TOP FOR AN EXTRA SALTY-UMAMI FLAVOR.

# EASY-ASS LASAGNA

Serves 8 • Prep Time: 5 minutes • Cook Time: 90 minutes • Total Time: 95 minutes

**Look, this isn't the most authentic lasagna in the world, but sometimes a cat doesn't have the sort of time a proper lasagna needs, ya know? This is a lasagna for when you're busy and hungry but still want something satisfying and delicious. Some say it's cutting corners: I say fuckin' take all the corners you want. Rules were meant to be broken. Forget the fuss of traditional lasagna—this version is all about getting those classic, cheesy, meaty layers on your table without breaking a sweat. Seriously, the prep time on this sucker is 5 minutes. Can you believe that? So, if you have a few minutes to spare and can do some other stuff for about 80 minutes to let this guy cook, prepare to be met with layers of cheesy, saucy goodness.**

## INGREDIENTS

1 pound (454g) 80/20 ground beef

½ teaspoon garlic powder, plus more to taste

¼ teaspoon onion powder, plus more to taste

½ teaspoon salt

¼ teaspoon freshly ground pepper

5 tablespoons unsalted butter

¼ cup all-purpose flour

1 quart (946ml) whole milk

9 ounces (255g) oven-ready lasagna sheets

1× 24-ounce (680g) jar marinara sauce

15 ounces (340g) ricotta cheese

1 cup shredded mozzarella

2 tablespoons grated Parmigiano Reggiano

2 tablespoons chopped fresh flat-leaf parsley, for garnish

### SPECIAL EQUIPMENT

9×13-inch (22×33cm) baking dish

## METHOD

1. Preheat the oven to 375°F (190°C).
2. In a big-ass bowl, mix the ground beef, garlic powder, onion powder, salt, and pepper.
3. Add the meat to a large pan over medium-high heat. Cook, breaking up with a wooden spoon, until brown, for about 8 minutes. Drain the excess fat and set aside.
4. Make the béchamel: Melt butter in a medium saucepan over medium-low heat.
5. Throw in the flour and whisk until silky smooth. Cook, stirring frequently, until the mixture has turned light gold but not brown, about 6 to 7 minutes.
6. Increase the heat to medium-high. Whisk in the milk and cook, stirring frequently, until thickened and smooth, about 20 minutes. Season, to taste, with a pinch or two of salt. It should be about as thick as thanksgiving gravy when you're done.
7. Place a layer of red sauce in the baking dish. Add a layer of pasta followed by a layer of béchamel and dollops of that luscious ricotta. Repeat starting with the red sauce, then the pasta, and so on until you've reached the top of the baking dish. Your final layer should be topped with red sauce and mozzarella cheese.
8. Bake, covered with aluminum foil, for 45 minutes. Uncover, sprinkle with Parmigiano Reggiano, and bake for an additional 10 minutes uncovered. Add the chopped pasrley, serve, and enjoy!

# COLORFUL-ASS TRI-COLOR PAN-SEARED LASAGNA

Serves 4 • Prep Time: 30 minutes • Cook Time: 1 hour 40 minutes • Total Time: 2 hours 10 minutes (plus 8 hours setting time)

**All right y'all, this one is a doozy. I'm not going to lie to you, this is a heavy lift, but man is it worth it. Don't get scared though, it's more time-consuming than difficult, but that's why it's a dish to pull out when you really want to make a statement. Think zesty pesto, an umami-rich red meat sauce, and a creamy ricotta sauce, tucked into layers and layers of lasagna noodles. Holy shit, I need a second....So if you're up to the challenge, grab your apron and get ready to make this bold and beautiful lasagna!**

## INGREDIENTS

### FOR THE RED SAUCE (MEAT MARINARA)

1 tablespoon olive oil
1 shallot, finely chopped
3 garlic cloves, minced
¼ pound finely diced pancetta
½ pound 80/20 ground beef
1 cup dry white wine
1× 28-ounce (794g) can crushed tomatoes (San Marzano)
1 teaspoon dried oregano
1 teaspoon dried basil
2 dried bay leaves
Salt and freshly ground pepper, to taste

### FOR THE GREEN SAUCE (PESTO)

⅓ cup pine nuts
2 cups loosely packed fresh basil leaves
½ cup grated Parmesan
½ cup olive oil
3 garlic cloves
Salt and freshly ground pepper, to taste

### FOR THE WHITE SAUCE

2 cups ricotta
½ cup whole milk
1 large egg
Salt and freshly ground pepper, to taste

### FOR THE LASAGNA

12 oven-ready lasagna sheets
½ tablespoon olive oil
Grated Parmesan

### SPECIAL EQUIPMENT

Food processor or blender
9×5-inch (23×13 cm) loaf pan

## METHOD

1 Preheat the oven to 375°F (190°C).

2 Prepare the Red Sauce: Heat 1 tablespoon of olive oil in a saucepan over medium heat. Add the finely chopped shallot and cook until translucent, about 3 minutes. Add the minced garlic and cook for 1 more minute.

3 Stir in the pancetta and the ground beef and cook, breaking up with a wooden spoon, until browned, about 5 to 7 minutes. Pour in the white wine and cook, stirring frequently, until very little liquid remains. This should take 3 to 5 minutes.

4 Stir in the crushed tomatoes, oregano, basil, bay leaves, salt, and pepper and simmer for 20 minutes, stirring occasionally. Remove bay leaves and set aside.

5 Next, prepare the Green Sauce: In a medium, dry skillet over medium heat, toast your little pine nuts until fragrant and golden brown, stirring constantly, about 3 minutes.

6 In a food processor or blender, pulse together the basil leaves, Parmesan cheese, olive oil, pine nuts, and garlic. Process that shit until smooth. If too thick, add a splash of water. Season with salt and pepper and set aside.

7 Next, prepare the White Sauce: In a large ass bowl, stir together the ricotta, milk, and egg until silky smooth. Season with salt and pepper, to taste, and set aside.

8 Grease the loaf pan with olive oil. Place a lasagna sheet on the bottom of the pan, making sure the bottom is fully covered. if one sheet is not wide enough to cover the bottom of the pan, use two sheets side by side. Spread an even layer of your meat sauce, about ½ cup (or enough to cover the noodles). Cover with another layer of lasagna sheets. Spread the top of the noodles with a layer of white sauce, about a ⅓ cup. Cover with more lasagna sheets, making sure it's fully covered. Add a layer of pesto, cover with noodles, and then repeat the layering (meat sauce, noodles, white sauce, noodles, and finally pesto and noodles. Finish by covering the last pasta sheet with marinara and sprinkling with cheese.

9 Cover with foil and bake for 45 minutes. Remove the foil and bake for an additional 15 minutes, or until the top is golden and bubbly.

10 Allow the lasagna to cool to room temperature. Cover and refrigerate overnight or for at least 8 hours—I know, this seems crazy, but you gotta trust me on this one.

11 Now it's time for the magic. Remove the lasagna from the bread tin and cut it into thick slices.

12 Heat a big-ass skillet over medium heat. Add a little bit of olive oil. Once shimmering, add the lasagna cheese-side down to the skillet. Cook for 2 to 3 minutes or until warm and gooey. Flip and cook 2 to 3 more minutes. Transfer to a plate, drizzle with a bit of olive oil and sprinkle with grated Parmesan cheese. Serve immediately and enjoy!

## CHEETAH'S SECRET

TO GET YOUR LASAGNA NICE AND DENSE, SET ANOTHER BREAD TIN ON TOP OF YOUR LASAGNA WHEN IT'S IN THE REFRIGERATOR. PLACE CANS OF FOOD IN THE EMPTY TIN TO ADD PRESSURE TO THE LASAGNA.

GOOD LUCK
BEATING
THIS MEAT

# GARLICY-ASS CHICKEN PITA POCKET

Serves 2 • Prep Time: 10 minutes • Cook Time: 8 minutes • Total Time: 18 minutes

**The only way you won't love this pita is if you have completely lost your sense of taste, or you're a vampire. Sure, there's tender, flavorful chicken tucked into a warm pita, but that's just the beginning. We're slathering on a garlic yogurt sauce so zesty, it's gonna have you singing a new showtune with each bite. This stuff is rich, creamy, and unapologetically garlicky—So, don't make any social plans for the next 24 hours, because your breath is about to enter beast mode. So, grab a napkin (or ten), and dig in. You'll thank me later—or hate me when you're brushing your teeth for the third time. Either way, it's worth it!**

## INGREDIENTS

2 medium boneless, skinless chicken breasts, cut into 1-inch (2.5cm) cubes

1 tablespoon dried oregano

½ teaspoon salt

½ teaspoon freshly ground pepper

2 cups plain non-fat Greek yogurt

2 tablespoons minced garlic

Juice of ½ lemon

1 teaspoon chopped fresh dill

1 teaspoon olive oil

Crushed red pepper flakes

2 pita rounds

1 small roma tomato, diced

¼ medium red onion, diced

### SPECIAL EQUIPMENT

Instant read thermometer

## METHOD

1. Season the chicken all over with dried oregano, salt, and pepper.
2. In a medium-ass bowl, mix the yogurt, garlic, lemon juice, dill, salt, pepper, and red pepper flakes. Taste the mixture and adjust seasoning as needed—sometimes a little extra lemon or salt makes all the difference.
3. Swirl the olive oil in a big-ass skillet over medium heat. Once hot, cook the chicken for 1 to 2 minutes on each side until golden brown and the internal temperature reaches 165°F (74°C). Remove from heat and allow the chicken to rest for 2 to 3 minutes.
4. Warm pita in a dry pan over medium heat, about 30 seconds each side.
5. Gently stir the chicken into the yogurt mixture and stir well to coat.
6. Cut open the pita, making a pocket. Place half of the chicken mixture inside along with half of the tomatoes and onions. Repeat with the remaining ingredients to make a second pita. Enjoy!

## CHEETAH'S SECRET

**TRY MY SUMAC ONIONS TO KICK THE FLAVOR UP A NOTCH.**

1 small red onion, peeled and thinly sliced

1¼ teaspoons ground sumac

1½ tablespoons red wine vinegar

Pinch of salt

1. In a medium bowl, stir together the onion, sumac, vinegar, and salt. Mix well.
2. Allow the mixture to rest at room temperature for at least 30 minutes. The onions will begin to soften and pickle.
3. Serve with your favorite dishes or as part of a salad.

# CHARRED-ASS CHICKEN SKEWERS

## with Cilantro Salsa

Serves **6 (2 skewers per person)** • Prep Time: **10 minutes** • Cook Time: **10 minutes** • Total Time: **20 minutes**

I was in San Francisco with a chef friend of mine, let's call her Stella. We decided to have some fun and do our own little version of a cooking competition like the ones you see on TV. So I brought what I thought were boring ingredients—chicken, cilantro, and Greek yogurt. Stella smirked as she started to break down a whole chicken. I thought, *"a'ight, maybe she's whipping up some pasta or a salad."* But no, she skewered up the chicken, coated it in spices, and then grilled them to perfection on her tiny balcony. I watched as she worked like a pro getting those perfect char marks, while I'm just sitting there, trying to act like I'm not already planning to propose. Then, she busted out this cilantro salsa out of thin air. I'm talking fresh, zesty, and with enough flavor to make you forget your own name. She drizzled it over the chicken like it was no big deal, but let me tell you, that salsa was a revelation. We sat down to eat, and I swear, every bite was bliss. We finished the meal, and let's just say the night didn't end with dinner. Those skewers weren't just charred—they were the prelude to a night that, much like that chicken, was deliciously hot and steamy.

### INGREDIENTS

- 2 tablespoons sweet paprika
- 2 tablespoons onion powder
- 1 tablespoon salt, plus more for seasoning
- 1 tablespoon freshly ground pepper, plus more for seasoning
- 36 ounces (1kg) boneless, skinless chicken thighs, excess fat trimmed and cut into 1-inch (2.5cm) chunks
- 1 small red onion, sliced into 1-inch (2.5cm) pieces
- 2 red or orange bell peppers, sliced into 1-inch (2.5cm) pieces
- 1½ cups fresh cilantro, leaves and stems
- 4 jalapeños
- 3 garlic cloves
- ¼ cup sour cream or full-fat plain Greek yogurt
- Juice of 1 lemon
- 3 tablespoons olive oil

#### SPECIAL EQUIPMENT:

- 12 wooden or bamboo skewers
- Blender
- Grill or grill pan

### METHOD

1. In a big-ass bowl, stir together the paprika, onion powder, salt and pepper. Add the chicken and toss to coat in the spice mixture.
2. Thread the chicken and vegetables on the skewers, alternating between the vegetables and chicken.
3. Add the cilantro, jalapeños, garlic, sour cream or yogurt, lemon juice, olive oil, salt, and pepper to the blender. Blend on medium until silky smooth, for about 2 minutes.
4. Preheat the grill to 450°F (232°C) or medium-high heat. Grill the skewers for about 2 minutes on each side, or until slightly charred and internal temperature reaches 165°F (73°C). (See Cheetah's Secret).
5. Drizzle or dip into sauce and enjoy.

# CRISPY-ASS CHICKEN KATSU

## over Rice

Serves 3 • Prep Time: 3 minutes • Cook Time: 10 minutes • Total Time: 18 minutes

**When I say crispy-ass, I mean you could hear this chicken crunch from the next room. Served over a bed of fluffy rice, this katsu is so perfectly cooked—so crazy crunchy—it sounds like one of those chiropractor ASMR videos. The combination is simple—fried chicken and rice. But when it's drizzled with chili crisp for a hit of heat and topped with scallions for that fresh-zingy kick, this dish is sure to give you a mouthgasm like no other.**

### INGREDIENTS

1½ cups short grain white rice
6 boneless, skinless chicken thighs
1½ cups all-purpose flour
2 large eggs, beaten
1½ cups panko bread crumbs
1½ cups high-heat oil such as canola or avocado
1 pinch of salt
3 tablespoons ketchup
1 tablespoon Worcestershire sauce
1 teaspoon soy sauce
1 teaspoon granulated sugar
3 tablespoons chili crisp
1 scallion, chopped

#### SPECIAL EQUIPMENT

Meat mallet or rolling pin
Cast-iron pan

### METHOD

1. Rinse rice under cold water until the water runs clear. Cook rice according to package directions (for best results, use a rice cooker if you have one).
2. In the meantime, trim excess fat from the chicken, then use a meat mallet or rolling pin to pound the chicken until it's ½-inch (1cm) thick.
3. Place the flour in a shallow bowl, add the eggs to another shallow bowl, and throw the panko crumbs into a third bowl of equal shallowness.
4. Working with one thigh at a time, dip the chicken in the flour and turn to coat. Next, dip the chicken in the egg. Allow the excess to drip off and then coat with panko, pressing gently to adhere.
5. Heat oil in a cast-iron pan over medium to medium-high heat. Once the oil is shimmering, add the chicken and cook for 3 to 5 minutes per side, or until golden.
6. Transfer to a wire rack and allow to cool for 2 to 4 minutes. Sprinkle with salt.
7. Mix together the ketchup, worcestershire sauce, soy sauce and sugar, stirring until the sugar is fully dissolved.
8. Slice your chicken into strips and place over rice. Drizzle with katsu sauce and chili crisp, and sprinkle with scallion, then serve hot!

### CHEETAH'S SECRET

USE A WOODEN SPATULA TO MAKE SURE THE OIL IS THE RIGHT TEMPERATURE FOR THE PERFECT COOK. IT WILL BUBBLE WHEN IT REACHES THE RIGHT FRYING TEMPERATURE.

## CHEETAH'S SECRET

**SERVE THIS WITH MY EASY LEMON-BUTTER SAUCE (BELOW) FOR A DECADENT TOUCH.**

¼ cup unsalted butter
1 garlic clove, minced
¼ cup chicken or vegetable broth
1 teaspoon Dijon mustard
2 tablespoons fresh lemon juice
1 teaspoon fresh lemon zest
Salt and freshly ground pepper, to taste
Chopped fresh flat-leaf parsley, for garnish

1. In a medium-ass skillet set over medium heat, melt the butter until it starts to foam. Add the garlic and cook, stirring constantly for about 1 minute, or until fragrant. Do not burn the garlic.
2. Pour in the broth, mustard, and lemon juice. Stir well to combine.
3. Let the mixture simmer for 3 to 4 minutes, or until it starts to thicken slightly.
4. Stir in the lemon zest. Season the sauce with salt and pepper to taste.
5. Sprinkle with chopped fresh parsley for garnish.
6. Drizzle the sauce over your prepared dish and serve immediately.

# SPATCHCOCKED-ASS CHICKEN

Serves 4 • Prep Time: 15 minutes • Cook Time: 55 minutes •
Total Time: 1 hour and 10 minutes (plus 24 to 48 hours air-drying time)

**Get ready for the chicken of your muthafuckin' dreams. We're talking spatchcocked chicken—flattened out like it lost a morbid game of twister—getting some VIP treatment in your fridge for two days. Why, you ask? Because air-drying this bird is the secret to skin so crispy, it's cosplaying as a potato chip. But we're not stopping there. Oh no, this chicken gets slathered in a garlic-herb butter so rich, it might as well come with a trust fund. By the time it's done, you'll have a golden, crispy, buttery masterpiece that'll make you feel like Gordon Ramsay. Enjoy it with applause when you serve it up—this bird is a showstopper!**

## INGREDIENTS

- 1× 4-pound, 8 ounce (2kg) chicken, rinsed and patted dry, giblets removed
- 3 garlic cloves, minced
- 2 to 3 fresh rosemary sprigs (minced)
- ½ tablespoon dried thyme
- 1 tablespoon salt
- 4 tablespoons unsalted butter, softened

### SPECIAL EQUIPMENT

- Large cast-iron pan
- Kitchen twine
- Meat thermometer

## METHOD

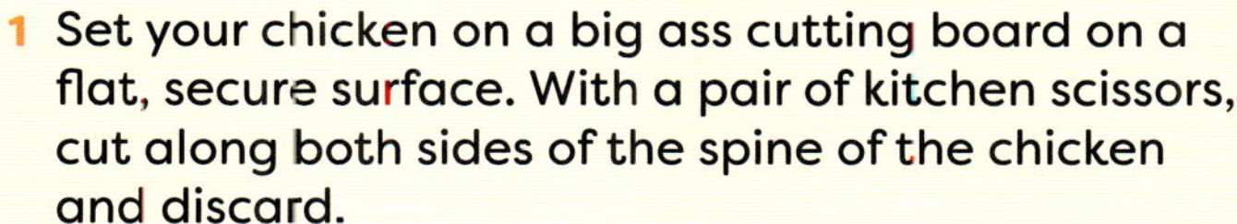

1. Set your chicken on a big ass cutting board on a flat, secure surface. With a pair of kitchen scissors, cut along both sides of the spine of the chicken and discard.
2. Flip the bird breast-side up. Place the palms of your hands over that juicy breast, and firmly press down until it busts wide open, allowing the chicken to lay flat.
3. Transfer the chicken to a sheet pan fitted with a wire rack then chill it in the fridge for at least 24 hours, or up to 48 hours. Being on a wire rack is really important so don't skip this—that way the air can reach every part of the chicken so it dries evenly, which will take your final product to the next level.
4. Remove the chicken from the fridge an hour before cooking and let rest on the counter. Preheat the oven to 425°F (220°C).
5. Place the garlic, rosemary, thyme, salt, and butter in a bowl and stir to combine. Set aside.
6. Rub the butter mixture all over the chicken and under the skin until fully covered.
7. Set the chicken in a large cast-iron pan. Tuck the wings underneath the body. Using kitchen twine, tie the legs together.
8. Bake that shit until golden brown or the internal temperature of the breast is 165°F (75°C), about 45 minutes. If you're an overachiever like me, baste the chicken with the juices after about 30 minutes. Once it's finished, remove from the oven and let rest for 10 minutes.
9. Cut that juicy, succulent bird however you like and serve it up!

# FRIED-ASS PORK CHOPS

## over Parsnip Puree with Roasted Fennel and Cranberries

Serves 4 • Prep Time: 20 minutes • Cook Time: 50 minutes •
Total Time: 1 hours (plus 2 to 4 hours arinating time)

I'm at this small, candle-lit bistro in Bavaria—the kind of place where you can practically taste the German ambiance. Across the room, I spot this stunning woman—think curvaceous goddess meets food critic. She's sitting there, effortlessly elegant, and somehow we strike up a conversation. Turns out, she's not just gorgeous; she knows her food. She leans in, eyes sparkling, and softly says, "You've never really lived until you've had the fried pork chops here." She orders for us, and when the dish arrives, it's a masterpiece. The pork chops are so perfectly fried, they've got a crispiness that could make even the most cynical skeptic believe in love at first bite. The parsnip puree is smooth, rich, and velvety, like the food equivalent of a slow jam. And those roasted fennel and cranberries? They add just the right amount of sweetness and tang, making the whole thing sing.

We share the meal, and it's like we're writing our own romantic comedy, one forkful at a time. So here it is, my homage to that night and that incredible woman: fried-ass pork chops that'll make you fall in love, parsnip puree that'll melt your heart, and roasted fennel with cranberries that'll keep you coming back for more. Enjoy responsibly—you never know where it might lead.

### INGREDIENTS

5 tablespoons kosher salt

4× boneless pork chops, 1-inch (2.5cm) thick

1 pound (454g) whole parsnips, cut into 1-inch (2.5cm) cubes

1 small yellow onion, quartered

3 tablespoons olive oil, divided

Salt and freshly ground pepper

½ cup whole milk

¼ cup heavy cream

2 tablespoons lemon juice

2 fennel bulbs, core and fronds removed, sliced into ⅛-inch (3mm) thick pieces

2 cups fresh or frozen (and thawed) cranberries

½ cup all-purpose flour

2 tablespoons garlic powder

1 teaspoon sea salt

1 cup oil with a high smoke point, such as vegetable

#### SPECIAL EQUIPMENT

Blender

Deep-fry thermometer

### METHOD

1 Add 4 cups of water and the kosher salt to a bowl large enough to fit your pork chops.

2 Submerge pork chops in the salt water, cover, and let rest in the refrigerator for at least 1 hour and up to 4 hours.

3 Meanwhile, preheat the oven to 400°F (200°C).

4 Add the parsnips and onions to a parchment-lined baking tray. Add 2 tablespoons olive oil and a pinch of salt and pepper and toss to coat.

5 Bake that shit until tender, about 25 to 30 minutes. It is fine if the vegetables char a little. Allow the vegetables to cool until cool enough to handle, about 2 to 3 minutes.

6 Add the parsnips, onions, milk and heavy cream to a blender and blend on low until silky smooth, about 2 to 3 minutes. Add the lemon juice, ½ teaspoon salt and ½ teaspoon pepper. Set aside.

7 In a medium-ass bowl, toss the fennel with 1 tablespoon of olive oil, salt, and pepper. Arrange in a single layer on a clean parchment-lined baking sheet. Cook for 10 to 12 minutes or until it starts to get some nice spots of char. Meanwhile, add the cranberries to another prepared baking sheet and bake for 5 to 7 minutes or until nice and plump.

8 Add the flour, garlic powder, and sea salt to a gallon-size zip-top plastic bag. Add the pork to the bag and shake until well coated.

9 Attach a deep-fry thermometer to a large, heavy-bottomed skillet. Add the oil and heat over high heat. Once the oil reaches 350°F (176°C), working with one piece at a time, remove the pork from the plastic bag, shake off any excess seasoning, and carefully place the pork in the pan. Cook for 5 to 6 minutes per side or until golden and an instant read thermometer reads 145°F (63°C) at the thickest part of the pork.

10 Serve pork atop the puree and top with the cranberries and fennel.

## CHEETAH'S SECRET

YOU CAN POUND YOUR PORK TO MAKE IT LOOK LIKE A MUTHAFUCKIN' SCHNITZEL. SIMPLY PULL OUT YOUR MEAT MALLET (NOT THAT ONE, NOAH) AND COVER YOUR PORK IN CELLOPHANE. USING AN OUTWARD MOTION AS YOU CAREFULLY SWING THE MALLET DOWN, FLATTEN AND WIDEN THE CHOP UNTIL IT'S ABOUT 1/3-INCH (8MM) THICK. CRACK A COUPLE EGGS INTO A BOWL, THEN WHISK, DIP YOUR PORK IN FLOUR, EGGS, THEN DIP INTO THE BREADCRUMBS. MAKE SURE THE BREADCRUMBS ARE CAKED ON NICELY THEN FRY IN 375°F (190°C) OIL FOR ABOUT 2 TO 3 MINUTES ON EACH SIDE OR UNTIL GOLDEN BROWN. LET IT REST ON A PAPER TOWEL-LINED DISH AND SPRINKLE WITH SALT AND SQUEEZE ON SOME FRESH LEMON JUICE.

# GREEK-ASS GRILLED TURMERIC LAMB CHOPS

## with Tzatziki

Serves 3 • Prep Time: 40 minutes • Cook Time: 8 to 12 minutes • Total Time: 52 minutes (plus 30 minutes for marinating)

I was backpacking through Greece, taking in the breathtaking views, when I found myself lost in the hills. Lucky for me, I stumbled upon a small sheep farm run by an old man named Nikos. This guy was the real deal—rough around the edges but with a heart of gold. After a long day of herding sheep (which, by the way, is way harder than it looks), Nikos decides to show me how they do dinner on the farm. He grabs some lamb chops, fresh from the flock, coats them in turmeric, oregano, garlic, and lemon, and throws them on a scorching-hot outdoor grill. When the chops are done, they're golden, with grill marks that look like they've been hand-painted by Da Vinci. I bit into one of the most succulent pieces of meat I've ever eaten and dipped it into a cool, creamy tzatziki sauce that took my taste buds to another world. We sat on the porch, eating straight off the grill and washing it all down with some homemade wine. It was one of the best meals of my life. So here it is, my take on a little taste of that Greek countryside.

### INGREDIENTS

2 tablespoons ground turmeric
4 garlic cloves, grated, divided
1 tablespoon dried oregano
Juice and zest of 1 lemon, divided
6 tablespoons olive oil, divided
Salt and pepper, to taste
6 lamb chops
1 cup grated cucumber
2 cups plain full-fat Greek yogurt
2 tablespoons chopped fresh dill, plus more for serving
Lemon wedges (optional, for serving)

#### SPECIAL EQUIPMENT

Grill
Instant read thermometer

### METHOD

1. Add the turmeric, half of the garlic, the oregano, half of the lemon juice, half of the lemon zest, 2 tablespoons of the olive oil, the salt, and the pepper to a zip-top plastic bag. Add the lamb chops and close the bag. Give the bag a shake to ensure the chops are evenly coated. Let them marinate at room temperature for 30 minutes. (If you want to marinate for longer, you can do so for up to 8 hours. Just make sure you put it in the fridge!)
2. Meanwhile, prepare the tzatziki. Place the cucumbers in a clean tea towel and squeeze out as much liquid as humanly possible. In a big-ass bowl, mix together the Greek yogurt, cucumber, remaining olive oil, remaining lemon juice, dill, and remaining garlic. Mix thoroughly. Cover and keep chilled until serving.
3. Preheat the grill to 450°F (230°C).
4. Grill the chops for 2 to 4 minutes on each side, or until the internal temperature reads 145°F (63°C) using an instant read thermometer. Allow the lamb to rest for 3 minutes.
5. Serve your chops with tzatziki on the side and garnish with remaining dill, and even a lemon wedge if you're feeling fancy!

# CHEETAH'S SMASHED-ASS BURGERS

Serves 4 • Prep Time: 5 minutes • Cook Time: 4 minutes • Total Time: 9 minutes

When someone says LA, what do you think of? Is it the Hollywood sign? Celebrities and influencers shopping on Rodeo Drive? Homelessness? Well for me, when I think of LA, I think of smashburgers. LA is famous for its smashburgers. Throw a coin, and you'll hit an aspiring actor who thinks they know where the best burger in LA is. They're probably right about it, too, because the city is teeming with incredible burgers. But there's no need to buy an overpriced plane ticket, because now you can make a killer smashburger in your own kitchen. So, grab your skillet, get it ripping hot like the California summer sun, and get ready to have your mind blown.

## INGREDIENTS

1 pound (454g) 80/20 ground beef
8 slices American cheese
2 tablespoons ketchup
2 tablespoons mayonnaise
1 tablespoon yellow mustard
1 tablespoon pickle relish
1 tablespoon salted butter
4 Brioche burger buns
1 large beefsteak tomato, cut into ¼-inch (½cm) slices
4 romaine lettuce leaves

## METHOD

1. Roll the beef into 8 evenly sized balls.
2. Preheat a cast-iron skillet on high. Lightly spray with avocado or canola oil.
3. Place 2 of those juicy balls in the pan and "smash" with a burger press (or the back of a spatula) until flat. Cook until nice and browned, for about 2 minutes until the edges are crispy and juice pools on the surface of the patty. Flip and add a slice of cheese to each patty. Cook 1 to 2 minutes more until the cheese is melted and set aside.
4. In a small bowl, stir together the ketchup, mayo, mustard, and relish. This will be your secret smashburger sauce.
5. Butter both halves of your buns and toast on the skillet until golden, about 1 minute (you can use the same one as before, just make sure it's not too dirty).
6. Spread the bottom bun with as much of your sauce as you like, then top with patties, tomato and lettuce. Serve and enjoy.

## CHEETAH'S SECRET

**TRY CHEETAH'S CHIPOTLE ZING SAUCE, IF YOU WANT A SPICY ALTERNATIVE TO THE SECRET SAUCE MENTIONED ABOVE.**

½ cup mayonnaise
2 tablespoons chipotle peppers in adobo sauce, minced
1 tablespoon fresh lime juice
1 teaspoon honey
½ teaspoon smoked paprika
1 garlic clove, crushed
Salt and pepper, to taste

1. In a bowl, combine the mayonnaise, chipotle peppers, lime juice, honey, smoked paprika, and garlic. Add salt and pepper to taste. Add more chipotle peppers or lime juice to make it extra tangy and spicy, if desired.

# BOMB-ASS STEAK SANDWICH

Serves 2 • Prep Time: 4 minutes • Cook Time: 7 to 11 minutes • Total Time: 15 minutes (plus up to 8 hours marinating time)

Picture this: You're holding a steak sandwich so good that even your vegetarian friend is eyeing that shit. This isn't just any sandwich; it's a culinary love letter straight from Argentina, sealed with a kiss of delicious chimichurri. We're talking juicy steak that's seared to perfection and slathered in a tangy, herby chimichurri sauce that's got more zest than your unmarried uncle after a couple margaritas. With creamy, gooey Havarti cheese to round it out perfectly, this sandwich isn't just food—it's an experience, a journey, and quite possibly the reason you'll need to buy bigger pants. Noah did (look at our older videos and you'll know what I mean).

## INGREDIENTS

1½-pound (680g) skirt steak
2 tablespoons Worcestershire sauce
2 tablespoons soy sauce
1 tablespoon salt
1 cup olive oil, divided
1 cup chopped fresh flat-leaf parsley
2 garlic cloves, chopped
1 small chili such as a jalapeño or serrano, seeded and finely chopped
½ tablespoon dried oregano
¼ cup red wine vinegar
2 ciabatta rolls
2 tablespoons salted butter
4 slices Havarti cheese

### SPECIAL EQUIPMENT

Kitchen torch (optional)

## METHOD

1 Place the steak in a gallon-size zip-top plastic bag. Pour in the Worcestershire sauce and soy sauce. Let marinate, refrigerated, for at least 2 and up to 8 hours.

2 Pull your meat out of the bag and pat dry with a paper towel. Season the steak all over with the salt. Add one tablespoon of olive oil to a big-ass pan set over medium-high heat. Once smoking, cook the meat for 3 to 5 minutes per side, then set aside to rest.

3 Add the parsley, oil, garlic, chili, oregano, and vinegar to a medium bowl and whisk that shit until combined.

4 Slice open the ciabatta rolls and butter the insides of the bread. Toast in a medium-ass pan set over medium-high heat until golden, about 1 minute.

5 Now, get out your bad-ass cooking equipment (a kitchen torch), lay two slices of cheese on the inside of the bottom piece of bread and torch that bitch until melted, about 30 seconds (see Note).

6 Slice your steak on the bias and lay on top of the cheese. Top with chimichurri and the other half of bread, cut in half and enjoy.

## CHEETAH'S SECRET

IF YOU DON'T OWN A KITCHEN TORCH, SET YOUR BROILER TO HIGH AND COOK UNTIL THE CHEESE IS MELTED, ABOUT 30 SECONDS.

# HAWAIIAN-ASS STEAK BITES

## over Rice with Grilled Pineapple and Onion

Serves 2 • Prep Time: 10 minutes • Cook Time: 18 to 22 minutes • Total Time: 28 to 32 minutes

I've been lei'd out a few times in my day, but nothing got me the way Leilani's steak bites did. We were at a cookout somewhere in Maui, drinking a few too many mojitos, when Leilani brought out her famous steak bites. I spent the rest of that afternoon begging her for the recipe, and she finally gave in. Now I make them all the time. Served up over rice with grilled pineapple, these steak bites will have you feeling the sand in your toes and the Hawaiian breeze in your fur.

### INGREDIENTS

- 1 cup white rice
- ½ cup light brown sugar
- ⅓ cup soy sauce
- ⅓ cup pineapple juice
- 2 tablespoons sesame oil
- 4 garlic cloves, minced
- 1 tablespoon grated fresh ginger
- 2× 10-ounce (283g) top sirloin steaks
- ½ teaspoon salt
- ¼ teaspoon freshly ground pepper
- ½ medium red onion, diced
- ½ fresh pineapple, peeled, cored, and sliced
- Sesame seeds, for garnish

#### SPECIAL EQUIPMENT

- Grill
- Instant read thermometer

### METHOD

1. Preheat the grill to medium-high.
2. Cook the rice according to package instructions. When finished cooking, set aside.
3. To make the sauce, add the brown sugar, soy sauce, pineapple juice, sesame oil, garlic, and ginger to a medium-ass saucepan set over high heat. Cook, stirring frequently, until the sugar has completely dissolved. Reduce the heat to medium-low and cook, stirring occasionally, until reduced and thickened to a syrupy consistency, about 10 to 15 minutes.
4. Season the steak all over with the salt and pepper. Add the diced onion and pineapple slices to one side of the grill and the steak to another. Grill the pineapple until juicy and charred, about 3 minutes on each side. Grill the steak for 3 to 4 minutes per side, until charred on the outside and cooked to desired doneness on the inside. Use an instant read thermometer to check the doneness, medium-rare is 145° (62°). Remove and allow the steak to rest for 2 to 3 minutes.
5. Cut the steak into bite-size pieces and add to the brown sugar mixture. Stir to coat.
6. Serve the pineapple and steak bites over the cooked rice and garnish with a sprinkle of sesame seeds.

# LOW-AND-SLOW-ASS CARNITAS

Serves 12 • Prep Time: 5 minutes • Cook Time: 8 hours 10 minutes • Total Time: 8 hours 15 minutes

Picture this: a hunk of pork butt, smothered in spices, cooked slowly in a little citrus and a lot of love (or laziness, your choice). Just set it and forget it, and by the time you remember you've got dinner going, the pork will be so tender it practically shreds itself. Stuff this juicy meat into a taco, put it on a salad, or hell, just eat it straight out of the pot with a fork. No judgment here. Just pure, delicious, slow-cooked perfection that'll make you look like a culinary savant, even if the hardest thing you had to do was plug in the slow cooker.

## INGREDIENTS

- 1× 3-to-4-pound (1.3kg-1.8kg) pork butt
- 1 tablespoon ground cumin
- ½ tablespoon dried oregano
- 1 tablespoon salt
- ½ tablespoon freshly ground pepper
- 1 medium white onion, sliced
- 5 garlic cloves
- 3 jalapeños, thickly sliced
- ¼ cup pulp-free orange juice
- 2 tablespoons Worcestershire sauce
- 2 tablespoons vegetable oil

### SPECIAL EQUIPMENT

Slow cooker

## METHOD

1. In a small-ass bowl, combine the cumin, oregano, salt, and pepper.
2. Now, rub your meat down until it's as seasoned as Michael Jordan on the wizards. Next, add the meat to a slow cooker. Add the onion, garlic and jalapeños. Pour in the orange juice and a splash of Worcestershire sauce. Set the slow cooker to low, cover and cook, and forget about it for 7 to 8 hours (see Note).
3. Transfer the meat to a cutting board and shred with two forks.
4. Add 1 tablespoon vegetable oil to a big-ass skillet over high heat, and spread out an even layer of the meat (you'll probably need to work in batches). Let cook for 7 to 10 minutes on high, flipping every two or so minutes so you get some nice, crispy pork bits. Serve in tacos, quesadillas, or any way you like!

## CHEETAH'S SECRET

IF YOU'RE IN A RUSH, YOU CAN SET THE SLOW COOKER TO HIGH FOR 5 HOURS INSTEAD FOR A QUICKER COOK.

# HARISSA-ASS GRILLED SHORT RIBS

Serves 6 • Prep Time: 45 minutes • Cook Time: 10 minutes •
otal Time: 55 minutes (plus 24 hours marinating time)

So I'm in Morocco, wandering through the medinas, getting lost in the maze of alleys when the smell of something incredible hits me like a ton of bricks. I follow my nose to this tiny, tucked-away café where this old Moroccan dude is cooking up something magical. Turns out, it's short ribs—slow-cooked, spicy, and dripping with flavor. He's using harissa, this fiery red paste that's like the soul of Moroccan and Tunisian cooking. It's smoky, it's got a kick, and it smells like it could wake the dead. The guy sees me drooling and invites me in. I sit down and he hands me a plate of the short ribs. The meat is so tender, it's practically melting into the dish. The harissa gives it this deep, rich flavor, with a slow burn that makes you keep going back for more, even though your mouth's already on fire. When I got back home, I knew I had to recreate this magic. So here it is: a little taste of Morocco, right in your own kitchen. Grilled until they're fall-apart tender, with all the smoky, spicy goodness you'd expect from something inspired by a backstreet Moroccan café.

## INGREDIENTS

### FOR THE HARISSA

- 2 chiles de árbol
- 10 to 15 dried red chiles (go for an even mix of guajillo, piri piri, and chipotle if you can, or just use whatever you have)
- 1 tablespoon, plus 2 teaspoons kosher salt
- 1½ teaspoons whole coriander seeds
- 1 teaspoon whole caraway seeds
- 1 teaspoon whole fennel seeds
- 1 teaspoon whole black peppercorns
- ½ teaspoon whole cumin seeds
- 1 cup extra-virgin olive oil
- 1 tablespoon sweet paprika
- 2 teaspoons hot paprika
- 2 teaspoons tomato paste
- 1 tablespoon chopped preserved lemon
- 2 tablespoons fresh lemon juice
- ¼ cup coarsely chopped white onion
- 10 garlic cloves, peeled
- ½ cup fresh mint, tough stems removed
- ¼ cup fresh dill, tough stems removed
- ¼ cup fresh marjoram, tough stems removed
- ¼ cup fresh flat-leaf parsley, tough stems removed
- 2 teaspoons honey
- 2 teaspoons dried ground mint (optional)
- 1 teaspoon ground sumac

### FOR THE SHORT RIBS

- 6 boneless short ribs
- Kosher salt
- Fresh scallions, cilantro, or mint, for serving (optional)

### SPECIAL EQUIPMENT

- Mortar and pestle
- Grill or grill pan

## METHOD

### FOR THE HARISSA

1. Toast the chiles de árbol and red chiles in a small, dry pan set over high heat, stirring frequently, for 2 to 3 minutes, until fragrant.
2. Transfer the chiles to a medium-ass bowl and cover with boiling water until fully submerged. Allow the chiles to soak for about 30 minutes.

3 Meanwhile, toast the coriander, caraway, fennel, peppercorns, and cumin in a small, dry pan set over medium heat, for 2 to 3 minutes. Transfer the spices to a mortar and pestle and grind into a fine powder.

4 Warm the oil in a small-ass saucepan, then add the ground coriander mixture, sweet and hot paprika, and tomato paste and cook, stirring constantly, until fragrant and the paste has darkened, about 10 minutes.

5 Drain the soaked chiles and throw 'em in a food processor. Add the preserved lemon, lemon juice, onion, garlic, mint, dill, marjoram, and parsley. Pulse until a coarse paste forms, about 2 minutes.

6 Add the chile paste to the saucepan with the tomato paste mixture. Stir to combine. Add in the honey, dried mint (if using), salt, and sumac. Cook over medium heat, stirring every 30 seconds, until homogenous, about 5 minutes. Let cool.

### FOR THE SHORT RIBS

1 Generously salt the short ribs and rub with three-quarters of the harissa. Cover and refrigerate for at least 12 and up to 24 hours.

2 Remove meat from the fridge and allow it to come to room temperature.

3 Preheat a grill or grill pan over high heat. Grill the short ribs until charred (3 to 5 minutes per side, depending on thickness, or until it reaches 145°F (63°C) on an instant-read thermometer.

4 Cover with foil and allow the meat to rest for 10 minutes. Serve with fresh or charred scallions, the remaining harissa, and cilantro or mint, if desired.

AYO

# SEAFOOD 'N' STUFF

# ZESTY-ASS SALMON POKE BOWLS

Serves 2 • Prep Time: 15 minutes • Cook Time: 25 minutes • Total Time: 40 minutes

This dish always takes me back to Hawaii, specifically this poke truck on the coast—no clue what it was called, but the flavors? Unforgettable. They were serving up poke so fresh and vibrant, it made you question why anyone bothers cooking fish in the first place. One bite and it's like your taste buds just woke up from a coma—zesty, bright, and exhilarating. And don't even get me started on the fluffy rice and all those killer toppings that made it filling, nutritious, and stupidly delicious. Seriously, don't sleep on making your own poke. It's crazy tasty, insanely easy, and trust me, you'll feel just like you're enjoying the breeze on a beach. Dive in and thank me later.

## INGREDIENTS

### FOR THE RICE

1 cup sushi rice

1 tablespoon rice wine vinegar

1 teaspoon granulated sugar

¼ teaspoon salt

### FOR THE POKE

12 ounces (340g) sushi-grade salmon, cut into 1-inch (2.5cm) cubes

½ tablespoon rice wine vinegar

1 cup light soy sauce

1 tablespoon sesame oil

Juice of 1 medium lemon

1 tablespoon granulated sugar

1 tablespoon sriracha

1 tablespoon toasted sesame seeds

1 teaspoon grated fresh ginger

2 scallions, chopped

2 cups veggies of your choosing (I enjoy shelled edamame, grated carrots, shredded purple cabbage, and diced cucumber)

½ ripe avocado, sliced into ⅛-inch slices

## METHOD

1. Rinse rice thoroughly, then cook according to package directions.
2. While it's going, grab a big-ass bowl and mix the vinegar, soy sauce, sesame oil, lemon juice, sugar, sriracha, sesame seeds, ginger, and scallions. Add the salmon cubes and stir to coat 'em up evenly. Cover the bowl and allow the mixture to rest in the fridge for 15 to 30 minutes.
3. Once the rice is done, scoop it into a second big-ass bowl. In a little-ass bowl, whisk together the rice vinegar, sugar, and salt until dissolved. Pour this mixture over the rice, and mix together using a spatula, allowing the rice to soak up all that deliciousness.
4. Grab two bowls and evenly distribute the rice, then top with the salmon. Top with your veggies of choice and the sliced avocado and welcome to poke-town!

# HOMEMADE-ASS BEET ROOT GRAVLAX

Serves **4** • Prep Time: **10-15 minutes** • Cook Time: **None** • Total Time: **10 to 15 minutes (plus 3 days for curing time)**

So I'm in Finland, where it's cold enough to freeze your tail off, but I didn't care because I was busy having a steamy fling with Annika, a tall, beautiful blonde with a kink for feeding me Nordic delicacies. One night, she introduced me to her not-so-secret lover—beetroot gravlax. I was lured into her kitchen by the smell of dill, citrus, and fresh fish. She pulled out this purple slab of salmon, and I'm thinking, "What the hell is this bloody mess?" But then she sliced it thin, laid it on rye bread, and topped it with fresh dill and a dollop of mustard sauce. One bite and I was hooked—like, considering-a-move-to-Finland-level hooked. The salmon was buttery, the beets added a sweet earthiness, and the dill graced it with an herbaceous undertone. Of course, we didn't last—turns out I'm not cut out for Finnish winters or a long-distance relationship. But Annika's beetroot gravlax? That stayed with me. Now, I make it whenever I'm feeling nostalgic or just want to impress someone with a taste of Scandinavia. Enjoy!

## INGREDIENTS

- 1× 2-pound (907g) sushi-grade salmon fillet, at least 1-inch (2.5cm) thick
- 2 purple beets, grated
- 2 serrano chilis (seeded and diced)
- Zest of 2 medium oranges
- 1 cup minced fresh dill
- ⅓ cup salt
- ⅓ cup granulated sugar
- 50ml vodka

## METHOD

1. Add the beets, chilis, orange zest, dill, salt, sugar, and vodka to a medium bowl. Stir until incorporated.
2. Place one-third of the beet mixture in a big-ass airtight container. Add the salmon on top of the mixture and then cover completely with the remaining mixture. Rest, covered, in the refrigerator for at least 60 hours and up to 72 hours.
3. Remove the salmon from the container, rinse under cool water, and prepare to be dazzled by the beautiful color.
4. Slice thinly, against the grain, and enjoy.

## CHEETAH'S SECRET

YOU CAN USE THIS RECIPE TO MAKE A BEETROOT GRAVLAX BRUNCH PLATTER TO STUN YOUR GUESTS. START BY SLICING YOUR GRAVLAX IN 1/8-INCH (3MM) SLICES AND FAN THEM OUT NEATLY ACROSS A BIG-ASS WOODEN BOARD. MIX AN 8-OUNCE (226G) PACKAGE OF FULL-FAT CREAM CHEESE WITH THINLY CHOPPED SCALLIONS AND MINCED FRESH DILL AND PUT IN A SMALL BOWL NEXT TO THE FISH. THEN, GET AN ASSORTMENT OF CRACKERS (I LIKE RYE CRACKERS AND BAGEL CHIPS) AND SLICED VEGETABLES (CUCUMBERS, TOMATOES, AND BELL PEPPERS ARE ALWAYS GREAT OPTIONS) AND LAY THEM AROUND THE PLATTER. FINALLY, SPRINKLE CAPERS AND FRESH DILL OVER THE WHOLE BOARD, AND YOU'LL HAVE YOURSELF A MAJESTIC BRUNCH CENTERPIECE.

# RAW-ASS TUNA TARTARE

Serves **4** • Prep Time: **10 minutes** • Cook Time: **None** • Total Time: **10 minutes**

I discovered tuna tartare in Monterey, California, and this shit was love at first bite. I was prowling around Cannery Row, soaking up the coastal vibes and hoping to snag some fresh seafood that wasn't deep-fried and served in a basket. I wandered into this swanky little spot overlooking the bay, where the ocean breeze had me feeling all kinds of fancy. The chef, a guy who looked like he surfed before every shift, suggested the tuna tartare. At first, I was skeptical—I mean, raw fish? I'm a cheetah, not a seal. But one bite and I was hooked: local tuna, diced and tossed in a sauce that was light, zesty, and delicious. Now, I can't go back to Monterey without hunting down some tuna tartare, and trust me, I've recreated it a million times since. It's like the perfect summer fling—refreshing, a little spicy, and something you'll never quite get over. So, here's my version: easy, delicious, and guaranteed to impress, whether you're by the bay or just dreaming of it.

## INGREDIENTS

- 1 pound (454g) fresh sushi-grade tuna, cut into 1-inch cubes
- 1 tablespoon dark soy sauce
- 1 tablespoon light soy sauce
- 1 teaspoon lemon zest
- 2 tablespoons chopped chives
- 1 tablespoon wasabi paste
- 1 tablespoon sesame seeds
- 1 teaspoon freshly ground pepper
- 1 avocado, peeled, pitted, and diced
- Microgreens, for garnish
- Crispy wontons or brown rice crackers (feel free to substitute any other cracker you like)
- Wedge of fresh lemon

## METHOD

1. To a big-ass bowl, add the tuna, soy sauces, lemon zest, chives, wasabi, sesame seeds, and pepper. Stir that shit up. Allow the mixture to rest at room temperature for 3 minutes.
2. Gently stir in the avocado.
3. To serve, shape the tuna mixture into a neat mound on a large plate. Top with microgreens and a squeeze of fresh lemon juice. Arrange wonton chips or crackers around the edges of the plate for dipping and digging in. Now enjoy that shit!

## CHEETAH'S SECRET

**KICK THIS DISH UP A NOTCH BY MAKING YOUR OWN WONTON CHIPS—JUST DON'T TELL ANYONE HOW EASY IT IS!**

- 1 package wonton wrappers, cut diagonally or into strips
- Vegetable oil, for frying
- Salt, to taste
- Garlic powder, sesame seeds, and chili flakes (optional)

1. Heat 2 inches (5cm) of vegetable oil in a deep pan or wok over medium-high heat until it reaches around 350°F (175°C).
2. Once the oil is hot, drop a few wonton pieces into the oil, making sure not to overcrowd the pan. Fry for 1 to 2 minutes, or until the chips are golden brown. Use a slotted spoon to remove the chips and drop 'em on a paper towel-lined plate to drain excess oil.
3. While the chips are still warm, sprinkle them with salt. You can also add garlic powder, sesame seeds, or chili flakes for extra flavor, depending on your preference.

# THE ULTIMATE-ASS TUNA MELT

Serves 2 • Prep Time: 5 minutes • Cook Time: about 6 minutes • Total Time: 11 minutes

It must've been around 3 a.m. at that diner in Wicker Park, the kind of place that feels like a warm hug after a night out in the cold Chicago winter. I'd just watched Xzibit tear up the stage with my friend Juliana, and we worked up an appetite bumping and grinding at the show. She always had this uncanny ability to order the best thing off any menu. Seriously, she could spot a hidden gem from a mile away. But when she ordered the tuna melt that night, I thought she'd finally lost it—or maybe we'd just had one too many cocktails. I gave her a look that screamed, "Are you kidding me?" and she just smirked, ready to prove me wrong. And, oh man, was I wrong. One bite and I was a believer. This was no ordinary tuna melt—it was a revelation. Creamy tuna salad with just the right amount of crunch from purple cabbage, piled onto crispy sourdough with cheddar cheese that melted like ice cream on a hot summer day. I made it my mission the next day to recreate that perfect sandwich, and I'm glad I did, because now I make this thing at least once a week. So grab some tuna cans and a spatula, and let's make the best tuna melt you'll ever have!

## INGREDIENTS

- 1× 5-ounce (113g) can albacore tuna in oil, drained
- ½ cup thinly shredded purple cabbage
- 3 tablespoons mayonnaise, divided
- 2 teaspoons Dijon mustard
- 1 teaspoon dried dill
- ¼ teaspoob salt
- ¼ teaspoon freshly ground pepper
- 4 slices sourdough
- 4 slices sharp cheddar
- Butter, for coating

## METHOD

1. In a medium-ass bowl, stir together the tuna, cabbage, 2 tablespoon mayonnaise, Dijon, dill, salt, and pepper.
2. Now this might seem strange, but trust me. Take the remaining tablespoon of mayo and spread it on the outside of two slices of bread. Turn the bread over and add a slice of cheese to each piece. Distribute the tuna salad evenly among the two cheese-covered slices of bread then cover each with the remaining slices of cheese. Top the sandwiches with the remaining slices of bread.
3. Heat up a large-ass skillet over medium heat and place the sandwiches buttered-side down in the pan. Press down on the sandwiches gently using a spatula to make sure the bread gets toasted evenly, and cook until golden, about 3 to 4 minutes. Flip and repeat, cooking until golden brown and crispy, about 3 to 4 minutes more.
4. Cut that shit in half and serve! I like to serve my tuna melt with kettle chips and a dill pickle spear like they do in a New York deli, but that's up to you.

## CHEETAH'S SECRET

ADD A LITTLE HOT SAUCE TO THE TUNA SALAD FOR A SLIGHT KICK. I USE TABASCO OR TAPATIO HOT SAUCE FOR THIS. ALSO, FEEL FREE TO USE YOUR FAVORITE CHEESE INSTEAD OF CHEDDAR!

# BEER BATTERED-ASS FISH TACOS

Serves 4 • Prep Time: 10 minutes • Cook Time: 10 minutes • Total Time: 20 minutes

**Sophia was a cheetah from Costa Mesa, California, and man, was she something else. I was just out there catching waves with the local cats when I spotted her little taco stand, barely more than a glorified shack by the beach. But while the stand wasn't much to look at, Sophia definitely was. She was slingin' these beer-battered fish tacos topped with a vibrant purple slaw and at just three bucks a pop, I figured she had to be losing money. But then I saw the line, and I realized she was probably rolling in it. Naturally, I grabbed three, and let me tell you, my taste buds went full Meg Ryan in *When Harry Met Sally.* I begged her for the recipe, but Sophia played coy; she said it was a family secret. So I cruised back up to LA with a belly full of tacos and a mission: recreate those bites of bliss. This is my take on Sophia's magical dish. Best enjoyed with the wind in your fur, sand in your paws, and a whole lot of meowing.**

## INGREDIENTS

2 cups shredded red cabbage
1 green onion, sliced
1 tablespoon apple cider vinegar
½ cup fresh cilantro leaves
1 cup all-purpose flour
1 teaspoon salt, plus more, to taste
1 teaspoon freshly ground pepper
6 ounces light beer
2× 6-ounce (170g) fillets of cod, cut into 4-inch (10cm) long strips
Oil, for frying
1 cup mayonnaise
Your preferred hot sauce, to taste
8× 6-inch (15cm) flour tortillas

### SPECIAL EQUIPMENT

Deep-fry thermometer

## METHOD

1. In a medium bowl, mix the cabbage and green onion. Add the vinegar and the cilantro. Gently stir to combine. Add salt, to taste, and set aside.
2. Next, make the batter. Stir together the flour, salt, pepper, and beer in a medium bowl. Thoroughly mix until no dry flour remains.
3. Attach a deep-fry thermometer to the side of a big-ass, heavy pan. Add 2 inches (5cm) of oil and heat to 375°F (190°C) over medium-high heat.
4. Working one piece at a time, submerge the fish in batter, shake off the excess, and add to the pan. Cook, undisturbed, until the bottom is golden, about 5 to 7 minutes. Flip and cook until equally golden and cooked through, about 5 more minutes. Repeat until all ingredients are used, being careful not to overcrowd the pan. You may need to work in batches.
5. Meanwhile, in a small bowl, stir together the mayonnaise and hot sauce.
6. To assemble, add 1 piece of fish to a tortilla, pile on some of the cabbage mixture, and drizzle with the spicy mayo. Enjoy!

## CHEETAH'S SECRET

**SERVE THIS WITH A DELICIOUS SPICY MANGO DIPPING SAUCE:**

1 ripe mango, peeled, pitted, and diced
¼ cup sweet chili sauce
2 tablespoons fresh lime juice
1 tablespoon honey
1 teaspoon soy sauce
1 small garlic clove, minced
½ teaspoon crushed red pepper flakes (optional)

**SPECIAL EQUIPMENT**

Blender or food processor

In a blender or food processor, combine the diced mango, sweet chili sauce, lime juice, honey, soy sauce, minced garlic, and red pepper flakes. Blend until smooth. Taste and adjust the seasoning if needed. You can add more honey for sweetness, lime juice for tanginess, or red pepper flakes for heat.

# SWEET-ASS COCONUT SHRIMP

Serves 4 • Prep Time: 5 minutes • Cook Time: 10 minutes • Total Time: 15 minutes

I was in a tiny fishing village in Barbados with some locals, having cervezas on the beach and exchanging stories at a little beach-side restaurant with no name. One of the guys I was with, Rudolfo, ordered us a bunch of appetizers. His brother, Servando, was the chef, and I'll be honest, I wasn't expecting anything mind-blowing going in. The spread consisted of the usual Caribbean seafood fare—good, but nothing to write home about. But then the coconut shrimp landed on the table, and with one bite, I was instantly transported to another dimension. The crunch of the breading, the sweetness of the coconut and the snap of the perfectly cooked shrimp was pure bliss. I thought they were perfect until Rudolfo told me to dip one in the spicy mango sauce. It was then I realized that this no-name restaurant in this little-known part of the Caribbean was on to some next level shit. I practically begged Servando for the recipe, and the dude was so chill, he scribbled it on a napkin without a second thought. When I asked if I could share the recipe in my book, Servando was all in, excited to spread the shrimp gospel. So here it is—straight from a hidden gem in Barbados and right to your kitchen. Get ready to taste a little slice of paradise!

## INGREDIENTS

- 2 large eggs, beaten
- 1 cup all-purpose flour
- 1¼ cup shredded unsweetened coconut
- ¾ cup panko bread crumbs
- ½ teaspoon salt
- ¼ teaspoon freshly ground black pepper
- 1 pound (450g) large deveined shrimp, tails on
- Oil, for frying

## METHOD

1. Add the eggs to a shallow bowl and the flour to another shallow bowl. In a third shallow bowl, stir together the coconut, bread crumbs, salt, and pepper.
2. Heat 1 inch (2.5cm) oil in a large-ass skillet over high until a pinch of breadcrumbs sizzles when dropped in (see Note).
3. Dredge the shrimp in the flour, then dip in the egg, shake off any excess, and roll it in the coconut mixture. Gently press that shit to make sure it sticks.
4. Cook until golden, about 1 minute per side. Serve with Cheetah's Spicy Mango Dipping Sauce (see page 162).

***Note:*** *This recipe also works with an air fryer. Simply spray the shrimp with olive oil and air fry at 450°F (230°C) for 5 to 7 minutes, or until golden brown.*

# SIMPLE-ASS TERIYAKI SALMON BITES

Serves 2 • Prep Time: 20 minutes • Cook Time: 7 minutes • Total Time: 27 minutes

Tokyo is a city that feels like stepping into a time machine that's stuck between ancient traditions and a neon-lit future. I was there diving into Asian flavors when I met Fumiko, a friend-of-a-friend chef on the west side. She insisted I try her teriyaki salmon and rice, and I thought, why not? She was stunning, the night was young, and I was in the mood for a culinary adventure.

She led me to her little hole-in-the-wall spot, where the ambiance was low key but the food was straight-up legendary. The dish was simple, almost unassuming—until I took a bite. That salmon, marinated in sweet teriyaki, was so buttery it practically melted like it was made of dreams and good decisions. The rice, soaking up all those juices, was next-level delicious. We spent the rest of the night drinking sake, swapping food philosophies, and talking until dawn. I had a train to catch, so we didn't, you know, take it to the next level, but let me tell you: the next time I'm in Tokyo, I'm making a beeline for Fumiko's teriyaki salmon.

## INGREDIENTS

2× 6-ounce salmon fillets, cut into 1-inch (2.5cm) cubes
¼ cup teriyaki sauce
1 tablespoon sesame oil
1 teaspoon honey
2 garlic cloves, minced
2 tablespoons dark soy sauce
Freshly ground pepper
Sliced scallions, for garnish
Sesame seeds, for garnish
Cooked rice and/or steamed vegetables of choice, for serving (optional)

### SPECIAL EQUIPMENT

Air fryer

## METHOD

1 Pat the salmon dry with a paper towel. Add the salmon to a large bowl with the teriyaki sauce, sesame oil, honey, garlic, soy sauce, and pepper. Stir until combined and the salmon is evenly coated. Set aside to marinate for 15 minutes.

2 Preheat an air fryer to 400°F (200°C). Add the salmon in a single layer and cook for 7 minutes or until the fish easily flakes with a fork.

3 Sprinkle with scallions and sesame seeds, then serve over rice or your favorite vegetables, or you can just devour them on their own for a delicious and healthy-ass teriyaki treat.

## CHEETAH'S SECRET

SERVE THIS WITH MY UMAMI-PACKED BROCCOLI: ADD 1 TABLESPOON OF AVOCADO OIL TO A LARGE-ASS PAN SET OVER HIGH HEAT, AND TOSS IN 3 CUPS OF CHOPPED BROCCOLI. IN A SMALL-ASS BOWL, WHISK TOGETHER 1 TABLESPOON EACH OF OYSTER SAUCE, FISH SAUCE, DARK SOY SAUCE, AND RICE WINE VINEGAR. ADD IN A CLOVE OF MINCED GARLIC AND POUR THE SAUCE OVER YOUR BROCCOLI AS IT FINISHES SAUTÉING—IT SHOULD TAKE ABOUT 5 MINUTES IN TOTAL. GIVE THE BROCCOLI A FEW TOSSES SO ALL THE PIECES GET COATED IN THE SAUCE AND SERVE IT UP PIPING HOT.

# BUTTERY-ASS GARLIC SHRIMP AND GRITS

Serves **4** • Prep Time: **12 hours** • Cook Time: **1 hour 3 minutes** • Total Time: **13 hours 3 minutes**

**Let me tell you, I never understood the obsession with shrimp and grits until I found myself in Savannah, Georgia, sweating like a sinner in church. I stepped into this little joint to escape the swelter and ordered the day's special: garlic shrimp and grits. When the server slid the bowl in front of me, I forgot all about the weather. This wasn't just food—it was a masterclass in simplicity: plump shrimp, sautéed in garlic and butter. I was halfway through the bowl when I realized this was the kind of comfort food that makes you want to curl up and purr. So here's my take on that magical dish. It's garlicky, buttery, and guaranteed to make you wonder why you haven't been eating this your whole life. The grits play backup like Meryl Streep in a supporting role, bringing a magnetic sophistication that will have you realizing a star is a star no matter the role.**

## INGREDIENTS

1 cup stone-ground grits
4 cups chicken stock
1 fresh bay leaf
¼ cup grated Parmesan
1 teaspoon salt
1 teaspoon freshly ground pepper
1¼ pounds (567g) raw, large shrimp (peeled and deveined, tails on)
5 tablespoons unsalted butter
4 garlic cloves, shaved
4 slices thick-cut bacon, cooked until crispy and crumbled
Fresh curly parsley, for garnish
2 teaspoons Louisiana-style hot sauce
Lemon wedges, for serving

## METHOD (SEE NOTE)

1. Add the grits and 32 ounces of water to a big-ass lidded pot and stir. Skim off everything that rises to the top. Soak overnight.
2. After soaking, skim the grits again and then drain the water.
3. In the same big-ass pot, add the drained grits, the chicken stock, and the bay leaf. Bring to a boil over high heat. Reduce the heat to low and simmer, stirring occasionally, for 45 minutes. Once the grits are looking nice and creamy, add the Parmesan and stir until melted and combined, cook for 10 minutes more. Turn off the heat, cover, and set aside.
4. Season the shrimp generously with the salt and pepper.
5. Melt 2 tablespoons of butter in a big-ass skillet over medium-high heat. Add the garlic and cook until fragrant, about 30 seconds. Add the shrimp and cook until opaque and pink, 2 to 3 minutes per side. Add the remaining butter and the hot sauce and cook for another 2 to 3 minutes.
6. To serve, plop a scoop of grits in a bowl. Top with half of the shrimp and finish with crumbled bacon, fresh parsley, and a squeeze of lemon juice.

***Note:*** *For this recipe, you'll need to start the grits the night before you cook the meal, so plan wisely young padawan.*

# CLASSY-ASS CLAMS

Serves **2** • Prep Time: **30 minutes to 1 hour** • Cook Time: **14 minutes** • Total Time: **44 to 72 minutes**

I learned to make this dish while I spent a week in Marseille. I was wandering the old port searching for seafood when I met Arun. He was a riot—a Thai chef with a knack for French cuisine and a spicy sense of humor that could rival mine. He invited me in for lunch, and I figured, why not? The place was barely bigger than a closet, but the smells coming from his kitchen were nothing short of divine. He whipped up these clams in a buttery white wine sauce that made me forget all about the fact I was in France being schooled by a guy who learned to cook from his grandmother in Bangkok. One taste and I was ready to declare my undying loyalty to both Arun and his clam sauce. The briny clams, swimming in a luscious pool of butter, garlic, and wine were delicious enough, but that kick of bird's eye chili and the fragrant basil took it to the extreme. I won't lie, I licked that plate clean like I was trying to bring it to climax. Arun was kind enough to pass the recipe on to me with a wink and a *"Don't tell my grandmother."* So, here it is—a French-Thai fusion you didn't see coming but won't be able to get enough of. Bon appétit, or as Arun would say, *"Eat up, cat-man!"*

## INGREDIENTS

2 pounds (907g) manila clams
3 tablespoons unsalted butter
2 garlic cloves, minced
1 medium shallot, minced
¾ cup dry white wine
½ cup heavy cream
Salt and freshly ground pepper, to taste
2 tablespoons roughly chopped fresh basil leaves, plus more for garnish
Lemon wedges, for serving

## METHOD

1. Soak clams in water for at least 30 minutes and up to 1 hour to remove all sand, then scrub any remaining dirt or barnacles. Nobody likes a sandy, barnacly-ass clam.
2. Melt the butter in a big-ass lidded saucepan set over medium heat. Add the garlic and shallot and cook for 1 to 2 minutes, until fragrant. Add the white wine, increase the heat to medium-high, and bring to a boil. Reduce the heat to medium-low and cook for 1 to 2 minutes more.
3. Add the clams, cover with the lid, and reduce the heat to low. Cook for 7 to 10 minutes. The clams are done when the shells pop open. Some will cook faster than others. Some won't open at all. It's all part of the game. Toss any that do not open once almost all the clams have opened.
4. Remove from heat and stir in the heavy cream, salt, pepper, and basil. Toss.
5. Garnish with more fresh basil and serve with lemon wedges to squeeze on top.

## CHEETAH'S SECRET

IF YOU DON'T HAVE ACCESS TO MANILA CLAMS, TRY LITTLENECK CLAMS OR MUSSELS INSTEAD. JUST NOTE THAT THEY HAVE DIFFERENT COOKING TIMES. USUALLY THE SMALLER THE CLAM, THE LESS TIME IT TAKES TO COOK! JUST LOOK FOR THE SHELL TO OPEN AND YOU'LL KNOW IT'S READY.

# MISO-ASS BAKED COD

Serves **2** • Prep Time: **5 minutes** • Cook Time: **6 minutes** •
Total Time: **11 minutes (plus 24 to 48 hours marinating time)**

Let me tell you about this bougie little number I discovered at a swanky restaurant in LA You know the type: the kind of place where the lighting is so dim that you can't see the menu, but you sure can see the prices. I'm sitting there in a room full of Instagram influencers and people who look like they don't pay taxes when the waiter brings out this tiny, artfully arranged plate of cod. The fish was flaky and tender, slathered in a miso glaze that was all kinds of sweet and salty. It was the kind of umami goodness that had me in seafood heaven—until I saw the bill. My options were clear: learn to make it myself or consider a side hustle I'd rather not mention. I chose the former, and after some trial and error, I'm proud to say I've nailed down the recipe. This is the type of shit that just needs to be shared with the world. It's easy, it's classy, and it won't have you choosing between dinner and rent. So go ahead, whip this up and treat yourself to a little taste of luxury without the credit card hangover.

## INGREDIENTS

¼ cup mirin
⅓ cup sake
⅓ cup white miso paste
⅓ cup granulated sugar
2 tablespoons rice wine vinegar
1 teaspoon grated fresh ginger
2× 4-ounce boneless, skinless cod fillets
4 chives

## METHOD

1. Bring the mirin and sake to boil in a small-ass saucepan over medium heat. Cook for 2 minutes.
2. Whisk in the miso and sugar and cook for 1 to 2 minutes, until the sugar dissolves. Set aside to cool.
3. Once the mixture is cooled, stir in the vinegar and ginger.
4. Add the fish to an airtight container, pour the miso liquid over it, cover, and refrigerate for at least 24 hours and up to 48 hours.
5. Preheat your broiler to high. Transfer the fish to a baking sheet and discard any extra marinade that hasn't been absorbed. Cook for 5 to 6 minutes. The fish should easily flake with a fork when done
6. Garnish by topping with chopped chives and serve with your favorite vegetables and/or steamed white rice.

# JERK-ASS FISH RECIPE

Serves 6 • Prep Time: 10 minutes • Cook Time: 15 minutes • Total Time: 25 minutes (plus 3 hours marinating time)

I was on a little getaway in Jamaica, chilling by the beach, soaking up the sun, and pretending I was on a Bob Marley album cover. The air was thick with the smell of ocean breeze, good weed, and that unmistakable jerk seasoning. I had the munchies, so I followed my nose to a smoky little shack that looked like it was held together by nothing but good vibes and duct tape. Behind the grill was this old Rasta dude named Winston, flipping fish like he was conducting an orchestra. He handed me a plate of jerk fish, and it was like my taste buds took a trip straight to Kingston and never looked back. The fish was tender and flaky, coated in a blend of spices so fiery it made me break a sweat. With the combination of allspice, scotch bonnet, and thyme, this dish can't help but taste spicy, bold, and insanely delicious. So here it is, my take on Winston's jerk fish, guaranteed to transport you straight to Jamaica without the airfare. Just don't blame me if you start craving Red Stripe and the sound of steel drums.

## INGREDIENTS

### FOR THE FISH

- 4× 4-ounce fish fillets (such as snapper, tilapia, cod, or mahi-mahi)
- 2 tablespoons olive oil
- 2 tablespoons fresh lime juice
- Chopped fresh cilantro or flat-leaf parsley, for garnish

### FOR THE JERK MARINADE

- 1 small white or yellow onion, roughly chopped
- 6 scallions, roughly chopped
- 3 garlic cloves
- 3 to 4 Scotch bonnet chiles
- 1 teaspoon ground allspice
- 1 teaspoon dried thyme
- 1 teaspoon ground cinnamon
- 1 teaspoon ground nutmeg
- 1 teaspoon ground ginger
- 1 teaspoon garlic powder
- 1 teaspoon onion powder
- 1 teaspoon cayenne pepper
- 1 teaspoon salt
- 1 teaspoon freshly ground pepper
- ¼ cup soy sauce
- ¼ cup fresh lime juice
- 2 tablespoons light brown sugar

### SPECIAL EQUIPMENT

- Blender
- Grill with grill basket (optional)

## METHOD

1. In a blender, combine all of the marinade ingredients. Blend for 2 to 3 minutes or until smooth and homogenous.
2. Add the fish to a big-ass baking dish. Pour the marinade over the fish. Cover and refrigerate for at least 2 hours and up to 6 hours—the longer you marinade the fish the more flavor you'll get.
3. Preheat the oven to 400°F (200°C) or fire up your BBQ if you want to grill this bad boy.
4. Shake any excess marinade off of the fish and toss the rest. Place the fillets on a baking sheet lined with parchment.
5. Bake (or grill the fillets in a grill basket) for 12 to 15 minutes, or until the fish is cooked through and flakes easily with a fork.
6. Transfer that shit to a serving platter, drizzle with olive oil and fresh lime juice, and garnish with chopped fresh cilantro or parsley.

# VEGETABLES, BUT NOT BORING

# GLAZED-ASS CARROTS

## with Parsley and Garlic

Serves 4 • Prep Time: 5 minutes • Cook Time: about 15 minutes • Total Time: 20 minutes

A dish that proves vegetables don't have to be boring, bland, or just that sad side dish nobody touches. I stumbled upon this little number at a vegan dinner party somewhere in the Hollywood Hills. You know how it goes—everyone's pretending they're into the kale salad while secretly waiting for dessert. But then, someone brought out these carrots, glistening like they'd just come back from a vacation in the Mediterranean. They were glazed with a buttery, slightly sweet coating, and then BAM—garlic and fresh parsley that hit me like a surprise party. I didn't think I could get this excited about a root vegetable, but there I was, shamelessly going back for seconds. So here it is, my take on simple and delicious glazed carrots with parsley and garlic!

### INGREDIENTS

1 tablespoon olive oil
1 garlic clove, thinly sliced
1 pound carrots, peeled and cut into 1-inch (½cm) pieces (see Note)
1 tablespoon maple syrup
1 teaspoon ground cayenne pepper
1 tablespoon unsalted butter
½ tablespoon fresh lemon juice
2 tablespoons roughly chopped fresh flat-leaf parsley
¼ teaspoon salt, plus more for sprinkling

### METHOD

1. Heat a big-ass pan over medium-low heat. Add the oil and swirl to coat. Once shimmering, add the garlic and cook until fragrant, about 30 seconds.
2. Add the carrots and 2 tablespoons of water and reduce the heat to low. Cook, shaking the pan frequently so it cooks evenly until carrots are just tender, about 10 to 15 minutes depending on the width of your carrots.
3. Pour in the maple syrup, drop in that butter and throw in the cayenne, stirring it all together. Cook for another 3 to 5 minutes until fully tender and the syrup thickens a little bit.
4. Garnish with parsley, squeeze on some fresh lemon juice, add extra salt, to taste, and serve.

### CHEETAH'S SECRET

FOR A REAL SHOW-STOPPER, TRY USING HEIRLOOM CARROTS IN A VARIETY OF COLORS. IF YOU'VE GOT EXTRA BABY CARROTS HANGING AROUND, THIS RECIPE IS A PERFECT WAY TO USE THEM UP—JUST BE SURE TO ADJUST THE COOK TIME SINCE THEY'LL COOK A BIT FASTER.

# EASY-ASS QUINOA TABBOULEH

Serves **4** • Prep Time: **15 minutes** • Cook Time: **15 minutes** • Total Time: **30 minutes**

**So, there I am, wandering the souks of Morocco, when I stumble upon this hidden restaurant—cool music, dim lighting, and a menu that's part poetry, part *"what the hell is this?"* Then, in walks Chef Amina. I watch her glide by me like she just stepped off of a magazine cover. We exchange a flirtatious glance, and before I know it, she's sliding a plate in front of me, leaning in close and saying, *"Taste this, habibi."* One bite, and I'm in tabbouleh heaven. It's light, fresh and zesty, with just the right amount of crunch. With the combination of parsley, mint, and tomatoes, it's like a rooftop garden party exclusively for my taste buds. And that quinoa? Fluffy as a cloud, soaking up lemon and olive oil like it found its true calling. Curious, I ask how quinoa found its way into her tabbouleh, and she casually mentions she has celiac and can't touch gluten without dumping like crazy. I brush off the TMI and keep the flirtation going. Celiac hadn't even crossed my mind as the reason why this recipe would be the way it is, but it works. So try this quinoa-based tabbouleh with enough charm to seduce anyone.**

## INGREDIENTS

1 cup quinoa

½ teaspoon salt, plus more to taste

1 cup finely chopped fresh flat-leaf parsley

1 cup diced tomatoes

½ cup finely chopped fresh mint

½ cup diced cucumber

¼ cup finely chopped red onion or green onions

¼ cup fresh lemon juice

¼ cup extra-virgin olive oil

Freshly ground pepper, to taste

## METHOD

1. Rinse the quinoa under cold water using a fine-mesh sieve. In a medium saucepan, bring 2 cups of water to a boil. Add the quinoa and salt. Reduce heat to low, cover, and simmer for about 15 minutes or until the water is absorbed and the quinoa is tender. Remove from heat and let it sit, covered, for 5 minutes. Fluff with a fork and let cool to room temperature.
2. In a big-ass bowl, combine the cooled quinoa, parsley, tomatoes, mint, cucumber, and onions.
3. In a small bowl, whisk together the fresh lemon juice, olive oil, salt, and pepper, to taste. Pour the olive oil mixture over the quinoa mixture and toss until well combined. Add more salt, pepper, or lemon juice, as needed. Serve with Cheetah's Fawaffles (see page 194)!

# ROASTED VEGETABLE SALAD

## with Honey-Chipotle Dressing

Serves 4 • Prep Time: 5 minutes • Cook Time: 30 minutes • Total Time: 35 minutes

This is a dish that says, *"Yeah, I'm healthy, but I still know how to party."* Now, we've all been there: staring at a sad bowl of lettuce, wondering why life has brought us to this point. But not today, my friend. Today, we're leveling up to make you forget every bland salad you've ever suffered through. We're talking sweet potatoes, broccolini, Brussels sprouts, and whatever else you got lying around—just throw that shit in. These veggies all get caramelized and crispy from the oven and come out looking like they've been sunbathing in the Sahara. You lay 'em on a bed of fresh curly kale, and then comes the star of the show: the Honey-Chipotle Dressing. It's sweet, it's smoky, and it's got a little kick to keep things interesting—like the perfect date, but edible. Drizzle that magic all over your roasted veggies, and suddenly, you've got a salad that's bold, sassy, and far from boring.

## INGREDIENTS

### FOR THE SALAD

- 3 cups curly kale, stems removed
- 1½ teaspoons salt, divided
- 1× 15.5-ounce (439g) can garbanzo beans, drained and dried
- 1 bunch broccolini, cut into 1½-inch (3.8) pieces
- 1 medium sweet potato, cut into ½-inch (1cm) cubes
- 1 cup Brussels sprouts, trimmed and halved
- 1 small red onion, thinly sliced
- 1 red bell pepper, deseeded and thinly sliced
- 2 tablespoons olive oil

### FOR THE DRESSING

- 1 chipotle pepper in adobo sauce
- 1 tablespoon red wine vinegar
- 1 tablespoon honey
- 1 teaspoon onion powder
- 1 garlic clove, peeled
- ½ teaspoon salt
- ½ cup plain Greek yogurt

### SPECIAL EQUIPMENT

Food processor or blender

## METHOD

1. Preheat the oven to 350°F (180°C).
2. Place the kale in a large bowl. Sprinkle with 1 teaspoon of salt and massage it into the kale for 1 minute. Set aside.
3. Add the broccolini, sweet potato, Brussels sprouts, onion, bell pepper, olive oil, and the remaining ½ teaspoon salt, to a sheet pan and toss to coat.
4. Roast for 20 to 30 minutes or until charred and tender.
5. Next, it's time to prepare the dressing. Add the chipotle pepper, red wine vinegar, honey, onion powder, garlic, salt, and Greek yogurt to a food processor or blender and process until silky smooth. If too thick, add water 1 tablespoon at a time.
6. Throw your kale into a big-ass serving bowl, then add the veggies, and top with dressing. Toss to coat and enjoy.

# ROASTED-ASS FINGERLING POTATOES

## with Parmesan-Parsley Sauce

Serves 4 • Prep Time: 5 minutes • Cook Time: 30 minutes • Total Time: 35 minutes

One night I was throwing a dinner party for some friends who thought a "side" didn't need to be any more exciting than a wet sponge, and I realized this was my chance to show them the light. So I halved the fingerling potatoes I got from the farmers' market, seasoned them and threw them in the oven. They came out looking like they just walked off a runway and were ready to catch everyone's attention. Most people would have been fine with them that way, but not me. I went ahead and smothered them in the creamiest, zestiest Parmesan parsley sauce my friends had ever experienced. Crispy on the outside, tender on the inside, and packed with flavor, this dish will have you saying goodbye to boring potatoes for the rest of your life. Serve them with the Spatchocked Chicken on page 135 for a perfect combination. You might want to snap a photo of this recipe because everyone is gonna be asking for it. Or better yet, tell those cheap mothafuckas to buy their own copy!

### INGREDIENTS

- 2 pounds fingerling potatoes, halved
- 2 tablespoons avocado oil
- 1 tablespoon salt
- 4 tablespoons olive oil
- 1 cup chopped flat-leaf parsley
- 2 garlic cloves
- 1 tablespoon freshly ground pepper
- 1 tablespoon fresh lemon juice
- 1 cup grated Parmesan, divided

#### SPECIAL EQUIPMENT

Blender

### METHOD

1. Preheat the oven to 400°F (200°C).
2. Arrange the potatoes on a baking sheet, drizzle with avocado oil, and sprinkle with salt. Toss to coat and then spread out into a single layer.
3. Bake for 40 to 50 minutes, or until the potatoes turn a nice caramel brown color. Transfer to a heatproof bowl.
4. Meanwhile, add the olive oil, parsley, garlic, pepper, lemon juice, and half of the Parmesan to a blender and blend on low until completely smooth, about 2 minutes. Add water 1 teaspoon at a time if the consistency seems too thick.
5. Pour half of the sauce over the bowl with the potatoes and gently toss until evenly coated.
6. Divide the potatoes between 4 plates, drizzle with the reserved Parmesan sauce, and sprinkle with remaining cheese.

### CHEETAH'S SECRET

BOIL THE POTATOES FOR 5 MINUTES IN LIGHTLY SALTED WATER BEFORE CUTTING THEM IN HALF FOR AN EVEN MORE TENDER FINISHED BITE!

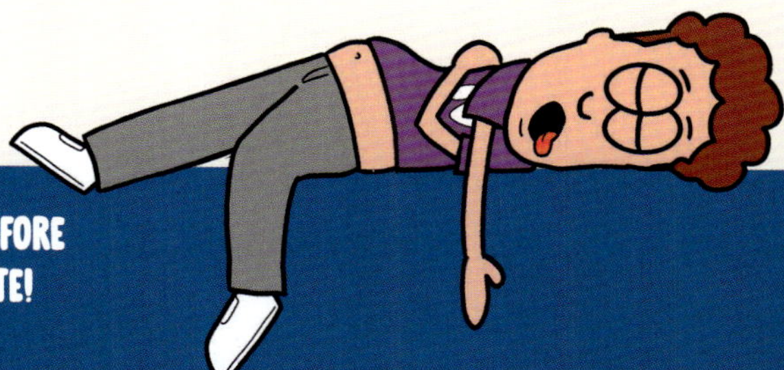

# HEALTHY-ASS SPAGHETTI SQUASH BOWLS

Serves 4 • Prep Time: 5 minutes • Cook Time: 50 minutes • Total Time: 55 minutes

So, there I was, having a charming evening with Shondra, until she casually dropped the "I'm vegetarian" bombshell. My heart sank faster than a soufflé in a wind tunnel. I quickly hid the brisket I had been smoking for 16 hours and looked in the pantry. Enter spaghetti squash: the superhero of the veggie world. I threw that bad boy in the oven, roasted it until it was tender and noodle-like, and then went to town stuffing it with beans, onions, and a sprinkle of cheese. The result? A meal that had her raving about how inventive and delicious it was. These bowls were so satisfying, she thought I had planned it out ahead of time. Now, these spaghetti squash bowls are one of my go-tos. They're the perfect mix of healthy, hearty, and satisfying.

## INGREDIENTS

### FOR THE BOWLS

2 medium spaghetti squash, halved lengthwise, seeds removed

1× 15-ounce (425g) can black beans, drained and rinsed

½ tablespoon garlic powder

Salt and freshly ground pepper, to taste

1 chopped medium red, orange, or yellow bell pepper

½ large white onion, diced

1½ cups shredded Monterey Jack cheese

3 tablespoons chopped fresh cilantro

### FOR THE SAUCE

½ cup chopped roasted red peppers (jarred or homemade)

2 tablespoons tahini

1 tablespoon fresh lemon juice

1 small garlic clove

Pinch of ground cumin (optional)

2 tablespoons olive oil

Salt and freshly ground pepper, to taste

### SPECIAL EQUIPMENT

Blender

## METHOD

1. Preheat the oven to 425°F (220°C).
2. Rub each piece of squash with oil, season with salt and pepper, and place on a baking sheet cut-side up.
3. Bake for 30 to 40 minutes or until fork tender.
4. While the squash is cooking, make the red pepper-tahini sauce by blitzing together all of the ingredients in a blender. If you feel like the sauce is too thick, thin it out with up to 2 tablespoons of water.
5. Mix together the beans, garlic powder, bell pepper, and onion in a medium bowl. Fill each piece of squash with one quarter of the mixture. Top with cheese.
6. Cook for 10 more minutes, until the cheese is melted and bubbling.
7. Top the squash bowls with as much sauce as your heart desires and garnish with cilantro.

# VEGAN-ASS CAULIFLOWER STEAKS

## with Cilantro Lime Avocado Sauce

Serves 4 • Prep Time: 7 minutes • Cook Time: 20 minutes • Total Time: 27 minutes

**I was in Lima, Peru, exploring a vegan gastropub that looked like it was designed by someone way too cool for their own good. I thought I'd be settling for "meh," when out came this cauliflower steak that would make a carnivore weep with joy. They had roasted the cauliflower until it was perfectly crispy and golden, with a texture so satisfying it could've fooled you into thinking it was a piece of gourmet meat. Then they hit it with a cilantro lime dressing that was so fresh and zesty, it practically danced off the plate. One bite and I was in vegan heaven. I was so blown away that I seriously considered sneaking into the kitchen to ask for the recipe, but I was too scared to piss off the chef. When I got back home, I was determined to recreate this masterpiece, and now I'm sharing it with you. So fire up the oven and get ready to be dazzled.**

### INGREDIENTS

#### FOR THE CAULIFLOWER

1 large cauliflower sliced into 1-inch (2.5 cm) "steaks"
2 tablespoons olive oil
1 tablespoon sweet paprika
1 tablespoon onion powder
1 teaspoon salt
½ teaspoon freshly ground pepper
½ cup pine nuts

#### FOR THE SAUCE

2 avocados, pitted and peeled
4 cups loosely packed fresh cilantro leaves
4 tablespoons fresh lime juice
2 garlic cloves
1 jalapeño, seeded
½ teaspoon salt

#### SPECIAL EQUIPMENT

Food processor or blender

### METHOD

1 Preheat the oven to 450°F (230°C).

2 Arrange the cauliflower steaks in a single layer on a baking sheet.

3 In a small bowl, whisk together the olive oil, paprika, onion powder, salt, and pepper. Brush both sides of the steaks with the olive oil mixture.

4 Bake for 10 minutes, flip, and bake for another 15 minutes, or until golden brown. Remove and let cool for 2 minutes.

5 Meanwhile, toast the pine nuts in a small, hot, dry pan over medium heat. Remove from heat after 2 minutes or when golden brown and fragrant.

6 Prepare the sauce: add the avocados, cilantro, lime juice, garlic, jalapeño, salt, and ¼ cup water to a food processor or blender and process until smooth. If too thick, add more water one tablespoon at a time until your desired consistency is achieved.

7 Distribute the cauliflower steaks among 4 plates and drizzle each plate with a ¼ of the sauce. Sprinkle with the pine nuts and serve.

# DELICIOUS-ASS DIJON-MISO-BUTTER SHISHITO PEPPERS

Serves **2** • Prep Time: **3 minutes** • Cook Time: **9 minutes** • Total Time: **12 minutes**

I was in Paris at a French-Japanese fusion spot, thinking I'd indulge in some classic French fare, when out came these peppers that changed my life. Blistered to perfection and tossed in a sauce of Dijon mustard, miso, and butter, these shishito peppers were like a flavor-bomb on a plate. The tangy, buttery, umami-rich sauce transformed them into something so addictive, I considered applying to work in the kitchen just to get the recipe. Back home, I spent weeks trying to recreate this taste of Paris, and I'm glad to say I figured it out. These peppers are earthy, buttery, and bursting with flavor, making you feel like you're dining in a chic fusion restaurant—even if you're just in your apartment kitchen. Get ready to impress yourself and anyone lucky enough to taste these delicious peppers!

## INGREDIENTS

- ½ pound shishito peppers
- 1 tablespoon white miso paste
- ½ tablespoon Dijon mustard
- ½ tablespoon red wine vinegar
- 3 tablespoons unsalted butter, melted
- Salt and freshly ground pepper, (optional, to taste)
- Juice of 1 small lime
- ½ teaspoon sesame seeds

## METHOD

1. Heat a medium ass pan over medium-high heat. Add the peppers and cook, stirring frequently, until they begin to char, which should take about 3 to 4 minutes.
2. Add the miso paste, mustard, vinegar, melted butter, salt and pepper, to taste (if desired), to a small-ass bowl and whisk thoroughly until well combined. Turn the heat to medium-low and toss that sauce in the pan, mixing it up well to make sure each pepper is coated (a little cheat code is to use tongs to grab and flip the peppers). Cook for another 2 to 3 minutes more, stirring often.
3. Turn off the heat and pour the lime juice over the peppers. Use a wooden spoon to scrape up and mix in any browned bits. Give it one last mix, then transfer the peppers to a serving bowl or platter. Sprinkle the sesame seeds, season with more salt and pepper, if desired, serve, and enjoy!

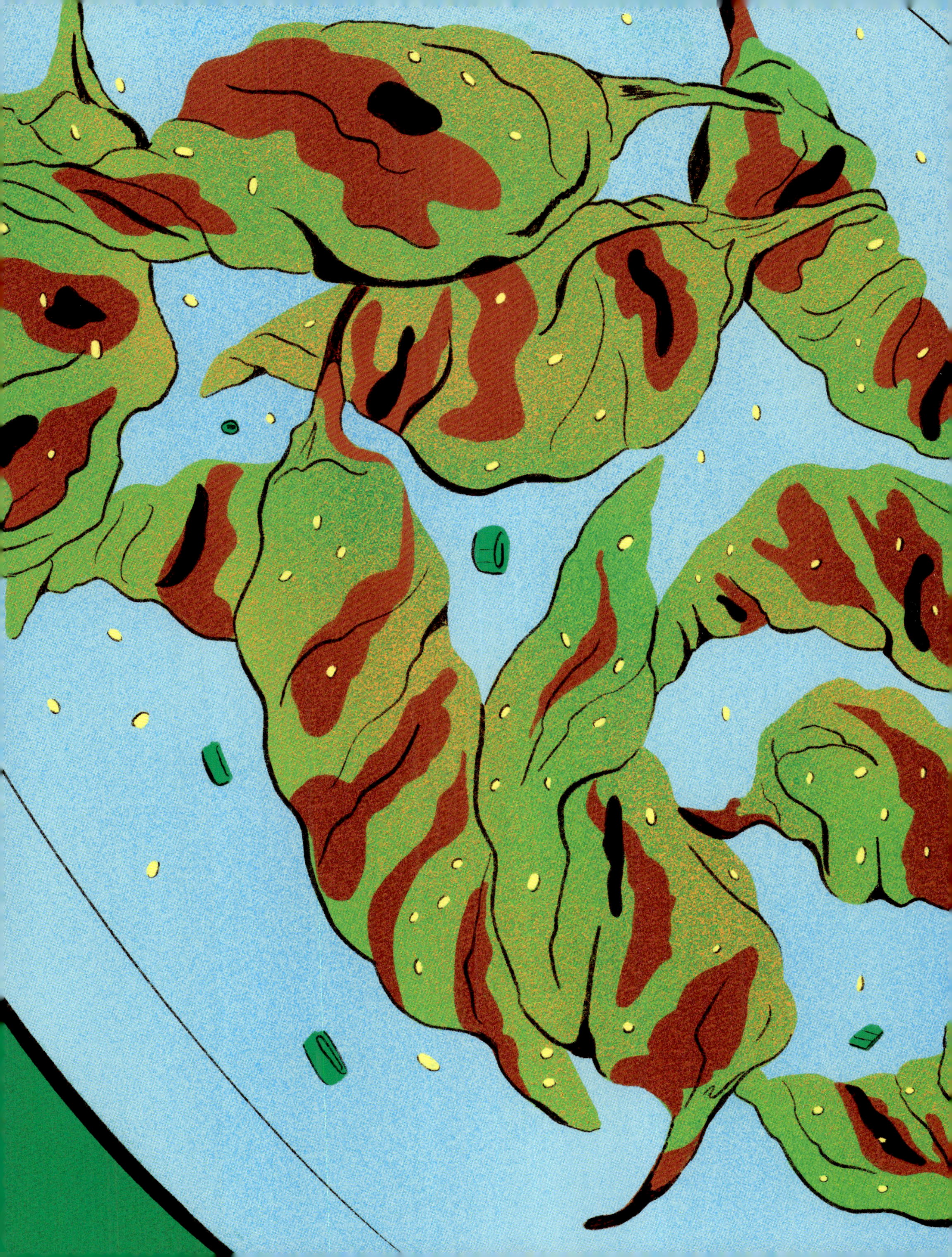

# EASY-ASS SHEET PAN ROASTED VEGETABLE POWER BOWL

Serves 6 • Prep Time: 7 minutes • Cook Time: 1 hour and 15 minutes • Total Time 1 hour and 22 minutes

Sometimes you need a meal that's as easy as it is tasty, especially on those nights when cooking feels like a monumental task. Enter the sheet pan—a game-changer for effortless deliciousness. I like to throw together whatever veggies are hanging out in my fridge—often potatoes, broccolini, carrots, and onions—onto a sheet pan. Then, I drizzle everything with oil, sprinkle it with spices, and let the oven work its magic. I like to finish my veg bowls with some tzatziki for a pop of tangy refreshment. The beauty of this power bowl is its flexibility. You can mix and match veggies based on what you have on hand or what's on sale. Bell peppers, Brussels sprouts, cauliflower—throw them all in and let the oven do the heavy lifting. It's a meal that makes you look like you've got your life together, even if you're just trying to avoid a last-minute dinner disaster. So next time you want a simple, customizable dinner with minimal fuss, this sheet pan roasted veggie bowl has got your back.

## INGREDIENTS

3 cups forbidden rice

Chicken or vegetable stock, for cooking the rice

1 large Japanese sweet potato, chopped into 1-inch (2.5cm) cubes (see Note)

1 large Yukon Gold potato, chopped into 1-inch (2.5cm) cubes

1 pound medium carrots, peeled and tops removed

1 bunch of broccolini, ends trimmed

1 medium yellow onion, sliced

1 tablespoon garlic powder

1 tablespoon ground turmeric

1 tablespoon paprika

¼ teaspoon salt

¼ teaspoon freshly ground pepper

2 tablespoons olive oil

12 ounces (340g) tzatziki (see page 139)

2 tablespoons chopped fresh flat-leaf parsley

## METHOD

1. Cook rice according to package directions, but swap the boring-ass water for chicken or vegetable stock, it should take about 30 to 35 minutes. Let the rice sit for 5 minutes, covered, after it's done.
2. Meanwhile, preheat the oven to 375°F (190°C). Line a baking sheet with parchment paper.
3. Place all vegetables, spices, and oil on the prepared baking sheet and toss to coat.
4. Roast that shit for 20 minutes, toss, return to the oven, and cook for 15 to 20 more minutes until tender and golden brown.
5. Divide the rice between 6 bowls. Top with vegetables and tzatziki, garnish with parsley, and serve.

### CHEETAH'S SECRET

JAPANESE SWEET POTATOES TYPICALLY HAVE A REDDISH-PURPLE SKIN AND WHITE FLESH. THEY'RE SLIGHTLY STARCHIER THAN THE ORANGE VARIETY AND ROAST BEAUTIFULLY. FEEL FREE TO SUBSTITUTE WITH ANY TYPE OF SWEET POTATO YOU PREFER.

# FANTASTIC-ASS FAWAFFLE

Serves 6 • Prep Time: 10 minutes • Cook Time: 15 minutes • Total Time: 25 minutes (plus 24 hours soaking time)

You ever have that crazy desire for Middle Eastern food, while at the same time craving the joy of eating a waffle? No? Just me? Well, it's gonna hit you in the face every few days the way it does to me ever since I stumbled upon this dish. Imagine biting into those crispy edges, the soft, herby center, and then, oh yeah, that drizzle of tahini sauce that nuzzled its way into every waffly indentation. It's all the familiar falafel flavors you love, but with the undeniable experience of a waffle—perfectly balanced, as all things should be.

## INGREDIENTS

1 cup dried chickpeas
2 garlic cloves
1 cup fresh flat-leaf parsley
1 cup fresh cilantro
1 teaspoon cumin powder
1 teaspoon coriander powder
1 teaspoon salt
1 tablespoon flour (or chickpea flour for gluten free)
½ teaspoon baking powder
Cooking spray
Tahini, for serving
Lemon wedges, for serving
Tabbouleh, fattoush, or baba ganoush (optional, for serving)

### SPECIAL EQUIPMENT

Food processor
Waffle iron

## METHOD

1 Rinse the chickpeas in cold water to remove any debris, then soak the chickpeas in a big-ass bowl with cold water. Make sure there's at least 2 inches (5cm) of water above the chickpeas, 'cause those muthafuckas will expand. Drain after 24 hours.

2 In a food processor, pulse the chickpeas, garlic, parsley, cilantro, cumin, coriander, and salt until a crumbly mixture forms that holds together when squeezed.

3 Add baking powder and flour to the mixture and pulse for another 15 seconds.

4 Preheat your waffle iron and spray both sides with cooking spray.

5 Spoon ½ cup of the mixture into the iron, and cook until golden for 2 to 3 minutes. If you'd like your waffle extra crispy, whip out the air fryer and preheat it to 375°F (190°C). Toss the waffles in and cook until crispy, about 3 to 5 minutes.

6 Serve with tabbouleh, fattoush, and/or baba ganoush, and a drizzle of tahini and lemon wedges.

## CHEETAH'S SECRET

**I LIKE TO SERVE THIS WITH MY EASY TABBOULEH RECIPE (SEE PAGE 181).**

**MAKE FAWAFFLE SLIDERS FOR A PERFECT PARTY APPETIZER.**

Make some mini fawaffles in your waffle maker by spooning 2 tablespoons of the mixture and cooking for 4 minutes. Grab some brioche slider buns and toast them up with a little butter for a minute on a hot pan. On the bottom bun, layer a crisp piece of lettuce, a juicy tomato slice and a tangy pickle. Add your freshly made mini fawaffle on top, then drizzle it generously with a creamy tahini sauce. Crown it with the top bun, and voilà—your fawaffle slider is ready to shine.

For the tahini sauce, mix ¼ cup of tahini with 2 tablespoons of fresh lemon juice, a minced garlic clove, and ½ teaspoon of ground cumin. Gradually whisk in 2 to 4 tablespoons of water until the sauce reaches your desired consistency, then season with a pinch of salt. The result is a creamy, tangy-ass topping that takes these sliders to the next level.

# SUCCULENT-ASS SWEET POTATO BAKE

## with Parsley-Tahini Drizzle

Serves 6 • Prep Time: 5 minutes • Cook Time: 52 minutes • Total Time: 57 minutes

**All right, so you've had baked sweet potato, but I guarantee you haven't had it like this. I'm talking tender, caramelized sweet potatoes, all roasted and golden, getting cozy under a drizzle of silky parsley-tahini sauce that's smoother than your best Tinder pickup line. This is the kind of dish that doesn't work hard but plays harder than Tyreek Hill on Sunday (shoutout to the other Cheetah). You can serve it up as a side, a main, or even just stand over the stove and eat it straight from the pan. No judgment here!**

### INGREDIENTS

6 sweet potatoes, cut into ¼-inch (½ cm) slices (use a mandolin if you have one)
3 tablespoons unsalted butter, melted
3 tablespoons olive oil, plus more for coating
1 teaspoon paprika
1 teaspoon chili powder
1 teaspoon salt, plus more, to taste
1 teaspoon freshly ground pepper, plus more, to taste
4 tablespoons tahini
2 tablespoons fresh lemon juice
¼ cup pine nuts
½ cup finely chopped fresh flat-leaf parsley

#### SPECIAL EQUIPMENT

12-inch (30.5cm) cast-iron skillet

### METHOD

1. Preheat the oven to 350°F (180°C).
2. In a small ass bowl, whisk together the butter, 2 tablespoons olive oil, paprika, chili powder, salt, and pepper.
3. Add the potatoes to a big bowl, drizzle with the butter mixture, and toss to coat.
4. Brush the skillet with oil. Lay the potatoes in a circle around the edge of the skillet, making sure they slightly overlap. Continue filling in the skillet with the potato, pressing the slices gently together so they're tightly packed. Cover with foil. Bake for 25 to 30 minutes, or until soft.
5. Uncover and brush with the remaining oil. Return to the oven and cook until golden brown, 10 to 20 minutes.
6. In a medium-ass bowl, stir together the tahini, lemon juice, salt, and pepper, to taste. Add in cold water 1 tablespoon at a time until the mixture is creamy and slightly runny (like the consistency of maple syrup).
7. Meanwhile, heat a small pan over medium heat. Add the pine nuts and toast, stirring often, until aromatic, about 1 to 2 minutes. Do not burn the nuts.
8. Drizzle tahini over potatoes, sprinkle with nuts and parsley, and serve.

### CHEETAH'S SECRET

**MAKE A SPICY AND SMOKY TAHINI DRIZZLE, AS AN ALTERNATIVE:**

¼ cup tahini
2 tablespoons fresh lemon juice
2 tablespoons adobo sauce
½ teaspoon smoked paprika
1 garlic clove, minced (optional)
½ teaspoon salt

1. In a medium bowl, whisk together the tahini, 4 tablespoons water, lemon juice, adobo sauce, smoked paprika, garlic (if using), and salt until smooth. The mixture might seize up at first, but continue whisking until it combines. If the tahini sauce is too thick, add a little more water, 1 tablespoon at a time, until you reach your desired consistency. If it's too thin, add a bit more tahini paste.
2. Taste the sauce and add more salt or lemon juice, if needed, to balance the flavors.

# VEGAN-ASS CHICKPEA CURRY

## with Coconut Milk

Serves 4 • Prep Time: 5 minutes • Cook Time: 23 minutes • Total Time: 28 minutes

So I was strutting the vibrant streets of Mumbai, when I stumbled upon a tiny, tucked-away eatery run by Priya, a vegan chef/model who was like Dumbledore in the kitchen. I was lured in by the intoxicating aromas wafting from her stove, and that's when she introduced me to this gem: Vegan-Ass Chickpea Curry with Coconut Milk. This curry's got all the Mumbai flair—bold, rich, and unapologetically packed with flavor. It starts with onions, garlic, and ginger sizzlin' in coconut oil, followed by a hit of spices that'll make your taste buds do a little Bollywood dance. In go the chickpeas, bell pepper, and peas, all bathed in creamy coconut milk and veggie broth. Toss in some spinach at the end for that healthy flex, and you've got yourself a curry that's as comforting as a warm Mumbai night. Priya taught me that this dish is all about flexibility—use whatever veggies you've got on hand, and if you're feeling carnivorous, throw in some meat. Serve it up with rice or naan, and let the magic of Mumbai's flavors transport you. Because a good curry doesn't just feed you; it makes you feel like you've discovered something special.

### INGREDIENTS

1 tablespoon coconut oil
1 medium white onion, finely chopped
3 garlic cloves, minced
1 tablespoon grated fresh ginger
1 tablespoon curry powder
1 teaspoon ground cumin
1 teaspoon ground coriander
½ teaspoon turmeric powder
¼ teaspoon ground cayenne pepper (optional)
1 red bell pepper, diced
½ cup frozen peas
1× 15.5-ounce (439g) can chickpeas, drained and rinsed
1× 13.5-ounce (400ml) can coconut milk
1 cup vegetable broth
2 cups baby spinach
Salt and freshly ground pepper, to taste
Chopped fresh cilantro leaves, for garnish
Cooked rice or naan bread, for serving

### METHOD

1. Heat the coconut oil in a big ass skillet or pot over medium heat. Add the onion and cook, stirring frequently, until translucent, about 5 minutes. Stir in the garlic and ginger and cook for another 1 to 2 minutes, or until fragrant.
2. Add the curry powder, cumin, coriander, turmeric, and cayenne pepper (if using). Stir well to coat the onions and cook until aromatic, about 1 minute.
3. Add the diced red bell pepper, peas, and chickpeas. Stir to combine and cook for 2 to 3 minutes.
4. Pour in the coconut milk and vegetable broth. Bring to a simmer and cook for 10 to 15 minutes, allowing the flavors to meld together and the sauce to thicken slightly.
5. Stir in spinach leaves and cook until wilted, about 1 to 2 minutes. Season with salt and pepper to taste.
6. Remove from heat and garnish with chopped cilantro. Serve it up nice and hot over cooked rice or with naan.

## CHEETAH'S SECRET

FEEL FREE TO SHAKE IT UP AND USE ANY VEGETABLES YOU'D LIKE. I TEND TO USE THIS RECIPE WHEN I HAVE TOO MANY VEGETABLES IN THE FRIDGE. YOU CAN EASILY ADD YOUR FAVORITE MEAT IF YOU WANT TO MAKE IT A CARNIVORE'S MEAL TOO!

# SWEET TREATS

# SWEET-ASS PUMPKIN LOAF

Serves 8 • Prep Time: 6 minutes • Cook Time: 60 minutes • Total Time: 66 minutes

Let me take you back a few years to one of those classic Ohio State vs. Michigan games. You know the ones—fans losing their minds, yelling at the TV like it's gonna change the score. So there I was, surrounded by all the usual game-day chaos, when I met Annie. She's this Columbus-based baker with a killer smile and an even better pumpkin loaf recipe up her sleeve. The kind of woman who shows up to a tailgate with baked goods that make you forget who's even winning. As a Michigan fan, I didn't want to like her baking, but after one bite that rivalry went straight out the window. See, Annie pulls out this Sweet-Ass Pumpkin Loaf, still warm, with a glaze that's glistening like it's showing off. One bite and BAM, I may as well have been a Buckeye. It's got everything: a loaf that's fluffy, moist, and packed with those fall spices that hit just right, and a glaze so smooth, you'll want to lick the bowl clean. Annie says it's her go-to for when she wants to impress without the stress, and honestly, I could see why—this loaf was scoring all the points. She tells me her secret is the orange juice, which keeps it moist and gives it a hint of tang. Pure stroke of genius if you ask me. So now, every time I whip up this Sweet-Ass Pumpkin Loaf, I think of Annie, her unbeatable tailgate treats, and that day I almost forgot I'm a Wolverine fan. Make this loaf and trust me, you'll be the real MVP of any tailgate.

## INGREDIENTS

### FOR THE PUMPKIN LOAF

Baking spray, for coating
1¾ cup all-purpose flour
1 teaspoon baking soda
1 teaspoon ground cinnamon
½ teaspoon ground nutmeg
½ teaspoon ground cloves
½ teaspoon ground ginger
¼ teaspoon salt
2 large eggs
1 cup granulated sugar
½ cup light brown sugar
1½ cups pumpkin puree
¼ cup pulp-free orange juice
2 tablespoons vegetable oil
1 cup semisweet chocolate chips

### FOR THE GLAZE

1 cup powdered sugar
1 cup whole milk
1 teaspoon pure vanilla extract

### SPECIAL EQUIPMENT

9×5-inch (23×13 cm) loaf pan

## METHOD

1. Preheat the oven to 350°F (180°C) and spray the loaf pan with baking spray.
2. In a big-ass bowl, mix together the flour, baking soda, cinnamon, nutmeg, cloves, ginger, and salt. Set aside.
3. In another big-ass bowl, whisk together the eggs, granulated sugar and brown sugar. Next, stir in the pumpkin, OJ, and oil.
4. Stir the wet ingredients into the dry until just combined. Make sure not to overmix!
5. Gently stir in the chocolate chips.
6. Pour the batter into the prepared pan and bake until deep golden brown and a toothpick placed in the center of the cake comes out clean. About 1 hour.
7. In the meantime, make the muthafuckin' glaze. In a medium-ass bowl, mix together the powdered sugar, milk, and vanilla until smooth.
8. Let the loaf cool slightly, then drizzle the glaze over the the top and serve.

# KUMQUATTY-ASS CARDAMOM LEMON BARS

Makes 24 bars • Prep Time: 30 minutes • Cook Time: 70 minutes • Total Time: 1 hour 40 minutes (plus 3 hours cooling time)

It was one of those summers in Malibu where the sun's always shining, the waves are perfect, and life feels like one big, glamorous daydream. I met this famous chef who lives out there—I can't say her name because of the NDA, but let's just call her a culinary legend. We had one of those whirlwind, only-in-Malibu kind of romances: beach bonfires, long dinners, and, of course, food that was just as unforgettable as she was. One night, she pulled me into her kitchen and said, *"I've got something special for you."* Out came these bars, and let me tell you, they were a revelation. A buttery, flaky crust that held up a zesty lemon-kumquat filling, laced with just enough cardamom to keep things interesting. She even topped them with these perfect little candied kumquats that shimmered like jewels, adding that extra touch of magic. It's got that perfect balance of sweet and tangy. And that hint of cardamom? It's like a warm hug that ties it all together, just like those Malibu nights. Every time I make these bars, I think back to that summer, that chef, and how much she made me Kum...quat Cardamom Lemon Bars.

## INGREDIENTS

### FOR THE CRUST

- 1¾ cup all-purpose flour
- ½ cup powdered sugar, plus more for decorating
- ¼ cup cornstarch
- 1 teaspoon salt
- 1 cup cold butter, cut into ½-inch (1cm) pieces
- 1 teaspoon pure vanilla extract

### FOR THE CURD

- ½ pint kumquats, halved and deseeded
- 6 large eggs
- 3 cups granulated sugar
- ⅔ cup all-purpose flour, sifted
- 2 tablespoons lemon zest
- ⅔ cup fresh lemon juice
- 2 teaspoons ground cardamom

### SPECIAL EQUIPMENT

- 9×13-inch (23×33 cm) baking dish
- Food processor
- Blender

## METHOD

1. Line the baking dish with parchment paper.
2. Add the flour, powdered sugar, cornstarch, and salt to a food processor and process for 10 seconds. Add in the butter and vanilla, and process that shit until a sandy texture forms.
3. Pour the flour mixture into the lined baking pan. Push the dough into the corners and up the sides of the pan by about ½ an inch (1cm). This will prevent the curd from leaking. Place in the fridge for 20 minutes.
4. Meanwhile, preheat the oven to 350°F (180°C).
5. Bake until the dough is golden brown along the edges and the surface is baked, about 15 to 20 minutes.
6. Add the kumquats to a blender and blend until pureed. If the mixture is too thick, add the lemon juice. Set aside.
7. In another large-ass mixing bowl, whisk together the eggs, sugar, flour, lemon zest, lemon juice (if you haven't used it already), the kumquat puree, and the cardamom.
8. Pour the curd mixture over the baked crust, then place back in the oven for 30 to 40 minutes, or until the top doesn't jiggle.
9. Let cool for 2 hours on the counter, then 1 hour in the fridge.
10. If desired, top with the candied kumquat slices and dust with powdered sugar. Cut into 12 equal-sized pieces and enjoy!

# PEACHY-ASS CRUMBLE

## with Ginger Whipped Cream

Serves 8 • Prep Time: 5 minutes • Cook Time: 36 minutes • Total Time: 41 minutes

It was a sweltering July in Georgia, where the peaches are sweeter than a first kiss and the humidity feels like you're walking through soup. I was cruising through the Peach State on a lazy summer road trip when I stopped at a roadside stand that promised the best peaches around. That's when I met Ella Mae, a Southern belle with a mischievous smile and a talent for turning fruit into pure poetry. She didn't just hand me a peach; she handed me the key to dessert nirvana: her Peach Crumble with Ginger Whipped Cream. Ella Mae swore by this recipe, saying it was passed down from her mama, who swore it could fix just about anything—from a broken heart to a sunburn. And after one bite, I believed it. The crumble was everything a summer dessert should be: juicy, sun-ripened peaches bubbling under a golden, buttery topping with just the right amount of crunch. And that ginger whipped cream? It's absolutely exquisite. Light, airy, and spiked with a touch of spice, it cuts through the sweetness and makes every bite sing. The secret, she said, was in using the ripest peaches you can find—the ones that practically fall apart in your hands. Toss them with a little sugar, cinnamon, and a squeeze of lemon, then top it all with a simple crumble of flour, butter, and brown sugar. Bake until it's all bubbling and golden, then serve it up with a generous dollop of that ginger whipped cream. So dig in, grab some sweet tea, and transport your taste buds to a summer night in the Georgia countryside.

### INGREDIENTS

- 6 ripe peaches, peeled, pitted, and sliced into ½-inch (1cm) pieces
- ½ cup granulated sugar, plus 1 tablespoon
- ¼ teaspoon salt
- 2½ teaspoons pure vanilla extract, divided
- ¼ cup all-purpose flour
- 6 tablespoons salted butter
- 1 tablespoon light brown sugar
- ½ cup rolled (old-fashioned) oats
- ¼ teaspoon ground cinnamon
- ¼ teaspoon ground nutmeg
- ½ sprig of fresh rosemary, finely chopped
- 1 cup heavy whipping cream
- 1 tablespoon ground ginger

#### SPECIAL EQUIPMENT

- 9×9-inch (23×23 cm) baking dish
- Handheld electric mixer or stand mixer, with the whisk attachment

### METHOD

1. Preheat the oven to 350°F (180°C) and grease the baking dish.
2. Add the peaches, ½ cup granulated sugar, salt, and ½ teaspoon of the vanilla to a large pot. Cook over medium-low heat, stirring constantly. Once the sugar has dissolved, transfer the peaches to the prepared baking dish.
3. Next, let's make the crumble topping. In a big-ass bowl, stir together the butter and flour. Mix in the brown sugar, 1 teaspoon vanilla, oats, cinnamon, nutmeg, and rosemary. Sprinkle the mixture evenly over those juicy peaches.

4 Bake until golden brown and bubbly, about 30 minutes.

5 Meanwhile, in a big-ass bowl, combine the heavy cream, 1 tablespoon granulated sugar, the ground ginger and 1 teaspoon of vanilla. Using a handheld electric mixer or stand mixer with a whisk attachment, whip until stiff peaks form, about 2 to 4 minutes.

6 Allow the crumble to cool slightly then enjoy topped with whipped cream.

## CHEETAH'S SECRET

TAKE THIS DESSERT TO ANOTHER LEVEL BY SERVING IT WITH FRENCH VANILLA ICE CREAM, TORN BASIL, AND OLIVE OIL.

# CHOCOLATEY-ASS BANANA BREAD

Makes 1× 9×5 inch (23×13cm) loaf • Prep Time: 10 minutes • Cook Time: 35 to 45 minutes • Total Time: 45 to 55 minutes

Let's talk about that sad bunch of bananas sitting on your counter, looking all speckled and ready for retirement. Wait! Don't throw them out, because we're about to turn them into Chocolatey-Ass Banana Bread that's so good, you'll wonder why you've been eating anything else for breakfast. Or lunch. Or, let's be honest, straight from the pan at 2 a.m. This recipe's got no time for frills—just mash up those overripe bananas, mix 'em with some melted butter, sugar, and a splash of vanilla, and you're already halfway to heaven. We're throwing in chocolate chips because this isn't your grandma's banana bread; it's banana bread with a glow-up. And the best part? You can toss it all together in one bowl. We're talking minimal cleanup with maximum satisfaction. Pour that luscious batter into a buttered baking dish, sprinkle a few extra chocolate chips on top (because fuck it), and let the oven do its thing. In 45 minutes, you've got a loaf that's moist, chocolatey, and practically begging you to slice off a thick piece.

## INGREDIENTS

- 4 overripe bananas
- ⅓ cup unsalted butter, melted, plus more for greasing (softened)
- ¾ cup granulated sugar
- 1 tablespoon pure vanilla extract
- 1 teaspoon baking soda
- 1 large egg
- Pinch of salt
- 1½ cups all-purpose flour
- ¾ cup semisweet chocolate chips, plus more for topping

### SPECIAL EQUIPMENT

9×5 inch (23×13cm) loaf pan

## METHOD

1. Preheat the oven to 350°F (180°C).
2. Grease the loaf pan all over with butter.
3. In a big-ass bowl, smash the bananas with a fork.
4. Add ⅓ cup melted butter to the bananas and stir.
5. Mix in the sugar, vanilla, baking soda, egg, and salt.
6. Add the flour and mix that shit up until no clumps remain. Don't overmix or you'll end up with a dense-ass loaf.
7. Gently fold in ¾ of the chocolate chips.
8. Pour the batter into the prepared dish and sprinkle with the remaining chocolate chips.
9. Bake for 35 to 45 minutes, until golden brown on top. and the batter doesn't jiggle when shaken. Give it the toothpick test—if it comes out clean, your bread is baked.

## CHEETAH'S SECRET

IF YOUR BANANA BREAD HAS BEEN SITTING OUT FOR A DAY OR SO, MAKE BANANA BREAD FRENCH TOAST. WHISK TOGETHER 1/2 CUP MILK, 2 EGGS, A PINCH OF CINNAMON, AND A PINCH OF SALT IN A SHALLOW BOWL. SOAK YOUR BANANA BREAD SLICES IN THE MIXTURE FOR 1 TO 2 MINUTES. HEAT UP SOME BUTTER IN A PAN OVER MEDIUM HEAT AND COOK FOR 3 TO 5 MINUTES ON EACH SIDE, OR UNTIL GOLDEN BROWN. SERVE WITH YOUR FAVORITE FRENCH TOAST TOPPINGS LIKE SYRUP, NUTS, OR MORE CHOCOLATE CHIPS!

# OOEY-GOOEY-ASS BROWNIE

Serves 12 • Prep Time: 10 minutes • Cook Time: 40 minutes • Total Time: 50 minutes

All right, this ain't your average brownie; this is the ooiest, gooiest brownie you'll ever make. We're talking fudgy, chocolatey bliss that's so rich, you'll feel like you need to check your stock portfolio after one bite. I first whipped these up on a rainy Sunday in Seattle when I was stuck inside with nothing but a craving and a lot of chocolate. The result? A tray of brownies so delicious, so perfectly sweet and chewy, I ate the whole tray myself without any milk. These bad boys bake up with a crispy top that gives way to the gooey center that'll make the most renowned French patisserie jealous. So go on, make these Ooey-Gooey-Ass Brownies when you need a dessert that's all about indulgence.

## INGREDIENTS

1 cup salted butter, melted, plus more for greasing

1½ cups granulated sugar

½ cup light brown sugar

4 large eggs

½ teaspoon vanilla bean paste (substitute ½ tablespoon pure vanilla extract, if desired)

1 cup all-purpose flour

1 cup unsweetened cocoa powder

Pinch of salt

4 ounces (113g) 56% dark chocolate, chopped

### SPECIAL EQUIPMENT

9×9-inch (23×23 cm) baking dish

## METHOD

1. Preheat the oven to 350°F (180°C) and grease the baking dish with butter.
2. In a big-ass bowl, mix the butter, sugar, brown sugar, eggs, and vanilla.
3. Sift in flour, cocoa powder, and salt. Whisk until incorporated.
4. Stir in the chopped chocolate.
5. Transfer the batter to the prepared baking pan and cook for 35 to 40 minutes, until crispy around the edges but still slightly wet (gooey) in the center.

## CHEETAH'S SECRET

MELT SOME CHOCOLATE CHIPS WITH COCONUT OIL AND DRIZZLE OVER THE COOLED BROWNIES FOR A CRUNCHY CHOCOLATE EXTERIOR. YOU CAN DO THIS WITH WHITE CHOCOLATE AS WELL TO MAKE A ZEBRA PATTERN EFFECT.

## CHEETAH'S SECRET

I LIKE TO TAKE TWO OF MY COOKIES AND FREEZE THEM FOR 10 MINUTES. THEN, I ADD 2 TABLESPOONS OF ICE CREAM TO THE FLAT SIDE OF ONE COOKIE AND PRESS ANOTHER COOKIE, FLAT-SIDE DOWN ON TOP OF THE ICE CREAM TO MAKE A CHOCOLATE CHIP COOKIE ICE CREAM SANDWICH. THIS IS ALWAYS A HIT AT PARTIES!

# DECADENT-ASS BROWN BUTTER CHOCOLATE COOKIES

Serves 12 • Prep Time: 10 minutes • Cook Time: 12 minutes • Total Time: 22 minutes

These aren't your run-of-the-mill chocolate chip cookies; these cookies got game. We're talking brown butter, baby—nutty, rich, and just slightly caramelized, bringing that depth of flavor like it's been cooking all day (but it's really just been about 5 minutes of browning over the stove while you try not to burn the house down). We start by browning the butter to perfection, then mix it with brown sugar and just a touch of white sugar because we like our sweets with a little dimension, ya know? Throw in a pinch of ground ginger to keep things interesting—don't worry, it's subtle but it's there, adding a little warm spice like a secret handshake. Stir in the chocolate chips, sprinkle some flaky salt on top (because we're fancy like that), and you've got cookies that are crispy on the edges, gooey in the middle, and straight-up irresistible. So, if you're in the mood for cookies that bring decadence and attitude, you've come to the right place. Life's too short for basic-ass cookies.

## INGREDIENTS

1¼ cups all-purpose flour
½ teaspoon baking soda
½ teaspoon salt
1 teaspoon ground ginger
½ cup unsalted butter
⅔ cup light brown sugar
¼ cup granulated sugar
2 large egg yolks
1 teaspoon pure vanilla extract
1 cup semisweet chocolate chips or milk chocolate chips
½ teaspoon flaky salt

## METHOD

1 Preheat the oven to 350°F (180°C) and line a baking sheet with parchment paper.

2 In a big-ass bowl, stir together the flour, baking soda, salt, and ginger.

3 Melt the butter in a small pan over medium-high heat. Once the butter begins to bubble, stir constantly, and cook until golden brown and fragrant, about 4 to 6 minutes. Make sure not to burn the butter. Transfer the butter to a heatproof bowl to cool slightly.

4 Add the butter, brown sugar, and sugar to a medium bowl and whisk until combined. Whisk in the egg yolks and vanilla.

5 Add the dry ingredients to the wet ingredients and stir until just combined. Gently fold in the chocolate chips.

6 Using a 2-inch (5cm) scoop or large spoon, drop rounded cookie dough balls onto the prepared baking sheet. You should have 12 dough mounds. Sprinkle with flaky salt. Bake for 10 to 12 minutes or until the edges are golden and set. Let cool and enjoy!

# NO FUSS-ASS TIRAMISU

Serves 9 • Prep Time: 15 minutes • Cook Time: None • Total Time: 15 minutes (plus 1 hour resting time)

If you've ever wanted to impress someone with a fancy dessert without actually putting in the work, this No Fuss-Ass Tiramisu is your new best friend. We're skipping the eggs, we're skipping the fuss, and we're diving straight into dessert glory in just 1 hour and 15 minutes. That's right, 15 minutes of work (and 1 hour of fridge time) to make something that looks like you've been spending all day in the kitchen, when really, you've just been chilling and sipping on that leftover espresso. Here's the game plan: whip up some cream with a touch of sugar, vanilla, and a splash of amaretto. Then dip those ladyfingers in cold coffee—don't overthink it, just a quick dunk will do—and start layering like you're stacking up the sweetest Jenga tower. Spread that fluffy whipped cream in between, dust the whole thing with cocoa powder, and boom—you're a dessert rockstar. The best part? No oven, no complicated steps, just pure tiramisu magic that's ready to chill in the fridge while you kick back and relax. Serve it up and let everyone think you've got some secret Nonna stashed in your kitchen making all the magic happen. They don't need to know it was this easy. Keep that part between us, and enjoy every creamy, coffee-soaked bite.

## INGREDIENTS

- 1½ cup heavy whipping cream, very cold
- ⅓ cup granulated sugar
- 1 tablespoon amaretto or brandy
- 1 tablespoon pure vanilla extract
- 1× 7-ounce (200g) package ladyfingers
- 1½ cups cold coffee or espresso
- Unsweetened cocoa powder, for dusting

### SPECIAL EQUIPMENT

- Handheld electric mixer or stand mixer
- 8×8-inch (20×20 cm) baking dish

## METHOD

1. Using a handheld electric mixer or stand mixer on medium speed, whip the very cold heavy cream, sugar, amaretto, and vanilla until soft peaks form, about 3 to 5 minutes.
2. Dip the ladyfingers in the coffee one at a time and arrange in a single layer on the bottom of the baking dish. Use half of your ladyfingers to form this bottom layer.
3. Spread half of the whipped mixture over the ladyfingers, then add another layer of dipped ladyfingers. Add the remaining whipped mixture.
4. Dust with cocoa powder using a mesh sieve and let sit in the fridge for at least 1 hour before serving.

# TOASTY-ASS BROWN BUTTER RICE CRISPY TREATS

## with Chocolate and Coconut

Serves 12 treats • Prep Time: 5 minutes • Cook Time: 15 minutes • Total Time: 20 minutes

So I'm in San Diego a few years ago on a perfect spring day. The sun's out, the waves are perfect, and I'm crashing at my buddy Jake's place—a total surfer dude with zero responsibilities because he lives with his grandma, who bakes like a rockstar. We walked into the kitchen after a long day of shredding the gnar. Immediately, we were enveloped by the overwhelming smell of brown butter and marshmallows. That's when I saw them stacked high on a plate—the most delectable array of rice crispy treats I'd ever seen. Nana Carol had a way of making everything feel like summer, and these treats were no exception. She told us she starts by browning the butter until it smells like caramel and makes you want to dive into the pan. Then she folds in the marshmallows, all melty and sticky, before stirring in the rice cereal. But she doesn't stop there—no, she knows how to live it up. She tosses in a handful of chocolate chunks and toasted coconut, because why the hell not? The coconut gives it that extra crunch and a hint of island vibes, like you're snacking on a beach with a piña colada in hand. So grab your ingredients, get that butter browning, and let these Toasty-Ass Brown Butter Crispy Rice Treats take you straight to that sunny San Diego state of mind.

### INGREDIENTS

- 10 tablespoons unsalted butter, plus more for greasing
- 1 cup sweetened, shredded coconut
- 6 cups mini marshmallows (or 5 cups if using regular size)
- ¼ teaspoon salt
- 6 cups crispy rice cereal
- 5 ounces (142g) dark chocolate chips

#### SPECIAL EQUIPMENT

9×5-inch (23×13 cm) loaf pan

### METHOD

1. Grease the loaf pan with a thin layer of butter.
2. Preheat the oven to 325°F (170°C). Line a baking tray with parchment paper.
3. Spread the coconut on the prepared baking sheet and bake for 4 to 5 minutes. Stir and bake for 4 to 5 more minutes or until golden. Set aside to cool.
4. In a big-ass pot over medium-high heat, melt the butter. Once bubbles form, stir constantly. Cook until golden brown in color and fragrant, about 5 to 7 minutes. Do not burn the butter. Remove from the heat and add the marshmallows. Stir until melted and silky smooth. Add cereal and stir to combine. Add most of the chocolate chips and coconut (reserving some of each for topping) and stir to combine.
5. Pour the mixture into the prepared loaf pan and press into the corners. Allow to cool slightly, then sprinkle on remaining chocolate chips and toasted coconut. Once fully cooled, cut into 12 equal pieces and serve.

# CHOCOLATEY-ASS BANANA IN A BLANKET

Serves **4** • Prep Time: **10 minutes** • Cook Time: **20 minutes** • Total Time: **30 minutes**

All right, so it's Thanksgiving, and I'm at my friend Maria's place—her big Italian family is out in full force. Cousins everywhere, Nonno asleep in the recliner with the game on, and Maria's mom yelling over the noise for someone to "stir the damn gravy." I'm just trying to stay out of the way, minding my business near the appetizer table, when Maria's Nonna walks in with this glint in her eye and a tray of something that's definitely not the standard Thanksgiving fare. Maria explained that her Nonna takes whole bananas, wraps them in buttery puff pastry, tucks in a little chocolate, and bakes them to crispy, golden perfection. It's like a portable little dessert bomb, and everyone knows Nonna's not playing around when it comes to sweets.

The second those pastries hit the table, the whole vibe shifts. Forget the turkey, the stuffing, the twenty different kinds of pasta—they're all lining up for Nonna's desserts. With that flaky, buttery pastry, gooey chocolate, and soft, warm banana, it had everyone from the littlest cousin to the loudest uncle swooning. Maria's Nonna just stands back, grinning, knowing she's crushed it once again. And you know, there's something kind of perfect about it—something that cuts through all the chaos of a big Italian Thanksgiving. It's sweet, it's simple, and it's delicious. So, if you find yourself at a holiday feast and the pies just aren't cutting it, grab some puff pastry, bananas, and chocolate, and channel a little Nonna magic.

## INGREDIENTS

- Flour, for dusting
- Half of a 1× (17.3-oz.) package frozen puff pastry sheets, thawed
- 2 ripe bananas, peeled and halved lengthwise
- 1× 12-ounce (340g) bar of your favorite chocolate
- 1 large egg, beaten
- Powdered sugar, for dusting

## METHOD

1. Preheat the oven to 400°F (200°C). Line a baking sheet with parchment paper.
2. Lightly dust a work surface with flour. Roll out the puff pastry sheet to smooth out any folds and ensure it is even. Cut the puff pastry into 4 equal squares.
3. Set a quarter of the chocolate bar to the side then roughly chop the rest of the bar.
4. Add roughly a tablespoon of the chopped chocolate to each of the pastry squares, arranging them in a diagonal line. Place a banana half on top of each pastry, covering the chocolate pieces.
5. Fold the sides of each pastry over the bananas and pinch the edges together to create a seam. They will look similar to pigs in blankets.
6. In a small-ass bowl, beat the egg with 1 tablespoon of water, then brush the top of each pastry with the egg wash. This will give the pastries a nice golden color when baked.

7 Arrange the pastries on the prepared baking sheet with at least ½-inch (1cm) space between them. Bake for 15 to 20 minutes, or until the pastries are puffed and golden brown.

8 Remove the pastries from the oven and transfer to a wire rack to cool.

9 Melt the remaining chocolate in the microwave in 10-second increments, stirring after each duration, until you get a runny chocolate sauce, and drizzle that shit over the pastries.

10 Dust with powdered sugar and serve!

## CHEETAH'S SECRET

CHECK OUT THE FULL PROCESS HERE, AS IT CAN GET A LITTLE CONFUSING.

TRY THIS!

# INDEX

## B

## D



## E

## S



## T

# ACKNOWLEDGMENTS

First and foremost, thank you to Noah—truly the best friend a Cheetah could ever ask for. To our friend Dan, without whom none of this would have been possible. A huge shout out to Stef Moser for capturing such evocative, mouthwatering photographs—your lens brings food to life. To Debs Lim, thank you for your stunning illustrations that added so much charm and personality to these pages. To Jake and Erica, thank you for graciously lending us your gorgeous (and, dare I say, sensual) kitchen for some of these shots.

Special thanks to Dante Kemble for your incredible support and collaboration in bringing these recipes together—you're a culinary MVP. Gratitude also goes to Molly Ahuja and the team at DK for taking a chance on a Cheetah like me; your belief in this project means the world.

Lastly, to my powerhouse team at UTA—Lisa, Brandi, and our brilliant managers Luke and Michael—thank you for always having my back. You all make chasing dreams feel possible.

With love and appreciation,

**CHEETAH**